ISBN: 0-89204-662-7

Acknowledgements

BY RON SMITH

Every book begins with a vague idea and blossoms into a well-defined collection of words, photographs and information. During the creative process, there are contributions from people who plan, edit, proofread, gather, process, design and assist in ways too countless to list. A lot of these tasks are performed by dedicated people who accept responsibilities beyond their weekly obligations.

It's difficult to imagine how the preparation of 61* could have proceeded without the vision of executive editor Steve Meyerhoff, who directed the project, assisted with the editing and provided behind-the-scenes encouragement. Or prepress director Bob Parajon, who pulled together the book's design and helped push it to completion.

Paula Kapfer executed that design and brought the Summer of '61 to life with a creative flair. Prepress specialist Chris Barnes-Amaro gave all the photographs his special attention and, with the help of Steve Romer, David Brickey and Vern Kasal, made them literally jump off the pages.

Special contributors to the editorial process were associate editor Dave Sloan, who took time out from his regular duties to proofread, and statistical editor Craig Carter, who kept an expert eye on the weekly home run charts while putting together the end-of-book Maris/Mantle comparison table.

◆

This book is broken down by weeks, which coincide with the publication schedule followed by *The Sporting News* in 1961. Week 1 has two extra days; Week 25 is three short. But the rest of the book is built around the information and box scores that were published in respective editions of TSN.

presents

61*

**The Story of
ROGER MARIS,
MICKEY MANTLE
and one
magical summer**

Table of Contents

Billy Crystal grew up in Long Island, N.Y., and has been a lifelong New York Yankees fan. He produced and directed HBO's film, 61*.

The summer of 1961 was the greatest of my life.

It seems like every game, every pitch, is on some sort of instant replay that I can't forget. Mantle and Maris ... Skowron and Berra ... Blanchard and Ford. Richardson to Kubek ... Boyer diving and throwing from his knees ... Ellie hitting . 348 ... Arroyo out of the bullpen ... Houk and the aviator glasses ... the ballpark.

It was the summer that everyone finally fell in love with Mickey Mantle, because Roger Maris was winning the race for the record. Ruth's record. Sixty. Mythical. Untouchable. If anyone should do it, it should be Mickey. He was supposed to be the one. It was his time, his ballpark. Who was this guy with the bad haircut, this flash in the pan? He shouldn't be the one.

Maris started the season slowly; Mickey was on fire. Then it happened. Roger got going, Mantle matched him; Roger went ahead, Mickey fought back.

We all started to take sides. This was serious. Someone was going to do it. Two Yankees going after Ruth. Perfect!

The Commissioner, Ford Frick, who had been a good friend of the Babe's, decreed that if anyone did break the record, he would have to do it in the same number of games in which Ruth did it (154). Otherwise, he said, it would have to carry a special notation.

Separate records. That stained the whole summer. On the day Frick's ruling was announced, ironically, Mickey and Roger both hit home runs that were not counted because of a rainout.

Maris would finish the 154-game season with 59 homers. With the pennant clinched, the press went after him. Maris was a .270 hitter; Babe hit. 340. He wasn't worthy, people believed. He had no flair, he was a bad interview, he never smiled. "Please, not him. We want the handsome, fun-loving Elvis in center field. He's the real Yankee."

Pressure grew. Maris got death threats. His hair fell out. Fans booed him in his own ballpark.

Why wasn't Roger what we wanted? He was, for two years, the best ballplayer in both leagues—the most complete. It wasn't enough. Why did he have to give more than what he gave on the field?

The day after Maris hit his 61st homer, a full-page ad in *The New York Times* from Macy's department store said there might be a new record, but the old record still stands. Maris is no Ruth.

Maris once said, "It was the greatest season of my life, but I wouldn't want to do it again." Well, it also was the greatest season of my life and, 40 years later, I've had the chance to do it again. This time as the director of 61*, to take people into the clubhouse, into the world of Roger and Mickey, the world I always imagined as a kid.

What I didn't know then was that Maris and Mantle had lived together that summer, sharing the ups and downs of the season, living the pressure together. While the press claimed they were feuding, they shared an apartment in Queens.

Roger and Mickey. The chase for Ruth's record. It's a great story of two teammates who became rivals and, ultimately, friends.

Billy Crystal

One stepped reluctantly into the New York spotlight in 1960, a naive, no-nonsense, tell-it-like-it-is small-town boy from Fargo, N.D.

The other had been auditioning for the role of New York icon for the better part of a decade, a handsome, fun-loving Oklahoma farmboy-turned-savvy sports star.

They were mirror images ... and polar opposites. Roger Maris and Mickey Mantle were connected in spirit by their common baseball goals, deep friendship and simple country roots ... and separated in history by their disparate outlooks on life and the epic battle they were forced to wage during one incredible season.

Soulmate sluggers in the Summer of '61

The same fate that brought them together as soulmate sluggers for the New York Yankees in 1960 also pitted them against each other a year later in a relentless media blitz that would define and redefine their careers. The Summer of '61 was pure theater with a fascinating plot and a diverse cast of characters—a national phenomenon that ripped apart one man's tender psyche and gave the other overdue status as a genuine American hero.

◆

Roger Eugene Maris was a simple man with simple tastes, ill-prepared for the blazing spotlight of New York City. The son of a North Dakota coal miner who instilled the traditional values of hard work, loyalty and dedication to craft, Maris never quite figured out why those working-class qualities did not play well in the fast lanes of the nation's sports media center.

It all seemed so simple growing up in Fargo, a friendly, slow-moving city of about 75,000 that is mirrored on the east side of the Red River

The summer of 1961 was pure theater with Mickey Mantle (left) and Roger Maris filling the role of leading men. Friends, teammates and soulmate sluggers, they worked in tandem to give fans one of the most exciting seasons in baseball history.

by Moorhead, Minn. Babe Ruth was merely a distant blip on Maris' radar screen. New York, home of the legendary Bambino and the mighty Yankees, was a million miles away from his 1940s reality of small-town America, complete with a Norman Rockwell innocence.

New York...was a million miles away from his...small-town America, complete with a Norman Rockwell innocence.

The one link to big-city sophistication was sports, and the Maris boys were blessed in that pursuit. Older brother Rudy was an outstanding high school athlete whose prospects eventually were dashed by polio. Roger exceeded Rudy's athletic prowess en route to becoming a local legend.

"I was a football halfback at Shanley (a Catholic high school), and I also played basketball and ran the dashes and put the shot in track and field," Maris told J.G. Taylor Spink, former editor of *The Sporting News*. "I had been an all-state halfback for two years. I led the state in scoring as a senior and helped Shanley win the North Dakota state championship as a junior. I had a lot of college scholarship offers and decided to go to the University of Oklahoma."

Shanley did not have a baseball team, so Maris carved out his future career in the regional Midget, Legion and City leagues. Cleveland scout Jack O'Connor was so taken with the 190-pound lefthanded hitter that he offered a $15,000 bonus, which was too good to pass up.

Maris settled his family into Kansas City life during his year and a half as a player there. It was a tie he would keep after his trade to New York.

"I wanted that college degree," Maris said, "but I asked myself, 'Would you be justified in passing up a lot of money in hand? You can help your family right now.' I signed with (the Indians). In 1953, $15,000 was a fortune for me."

Maris began his rise through the Indians organization by playing locally for Fargo-Moorhead, a local Class C team in the Northern League. It was during his second professional season, in the Class B Three-I League, that he met the man who would harness his vast talents.

"I started out as a spray hitter," Maris told Spink. "When I came to Keokuk (in 1954), I had the good fortune to work under a splendid manager, Jo-Jo White. He told me that I had enough power to pull for homers and so I changed my style. I hit 32 out of the park."

Maris, the favorite son of Fargo, N.D., was a natural for New York baseball, but adjustment to the big-city lifestyle was a huge struggle.

Welcome to... FARGO POPULATION 50,000 HOME TOWN OF— ...ARIS "The Home Run King"

A young Maris showed only flashes of his offensive talents during his year and a half with Cleveland.

By 1956, Maris had advanced to Indianapolis of the Triple-A American Association and a year later he was playing right field for Cleveland. He was fundamentally sound, fast, an excellent fielder and a dead pull hitter with explosive power. But Maris also was prone to extended slumps—and injury. His first big-league season was interrupted by two broken ribs, his second by a midseason trade to Kansas City and his third by an emergency appendicitis.

There were flashes of greatness (28 homers in 1958), but nothing to suggest Maris could ever match home runs with the likes of Mantle or Harmon Killebrew. There were whispers of attitude problems, but that traced primarily to differences with Cleveland manager Bobby Bragan that prompted the Kansas City trade.

Arms extended, muscles bulging, the Maris swing and intensity were perfect fits for the friendly right field porch of Yankee Stadium.

"If there is anything I am not, it is a Jake," Maris said when asked to explain his problems with Bragan in 1958. "I play hard, I train hard, I like baseball and I am determined to be somebody above the run of the mine. Imagine how I felt when Bragan called me in and said, 'Maris, I am fed up with your loafing.' ... Mr. Bragan did not know what he was talking about, and events soon proved that he didn't know."

Maris lashed back at Bragan and refused to back down, forcing a June 15 trade to the A's. Amazingly, Bragan was fired by the Indians less than two weeks later.

"I play hard, I train hard, I like baseball..." —ROGER MARIS

None of that seemed to bother New York manager Casey Stengel who, perhaps envisioning that quick, compact swing driving balls into the short Yankee Stadium right field porch, ignored the rumors and endorsed a trade that sent Hank Bauer, Norm Siebern, Don Larsen and Marv Throneberry to the Athletics in December 1959 for Maris, first baseman Kent Hadley and shortstop Joe DeMaestri.

"I don't know if I want to go to New York," Maris said only half facetiously after learning that he now belonged to the most storied franchise in baseball history. "They'll have to pay me a lot more money because I like it here in Kansas City."

The words zipped through New York like a shrill whistle.

◆

There never was any doubt that Mickey Charles Mantle would be a major league player. The swing, the instincts and the intensity were instilled early and groomed by his father, Elven "Mutt" Mantle, a frustrated sandlot star who supported his family as a zinc miner in the tiny community of Commerce, Okla. The elder Mantle worked out his son relentlessly, grilled him on fundamentals and insisted that he learn to switch hit, a tool that would serve him well.

Baseball was king in the Mantle household, which was located, ironically, in the heart of the football crazy Southwest. "I was a helluva football player," Mantle once said, but his days as a halfback for Commerce High simply marked time between the more important seasons of his life.

"I just wanted to please him more than anything," Mantle said, referring to the baseball dream he would live out for his demanding father. "I had so much respect for him."

...a perfect blend of physical skills and raw power.

Mantle also had talent, superstar-type talent that attracted Yankees scout Tom Greenwade. What Greenwade saw was a perfect blend of physical skills and raw power locked into a muscular, 5-foot-11, 195-pound body. His speed was extraordinary (3.1 seconds from home to first), his arm was strong and his instincts were uncanny. But more than anything, the Yankees were attracted by the unheard of power from both sides of the plate and a swing tailored to fit his thick $17\frac{1}{2}$-inch neck, powerful shoulders, strong back and bulging biceps.

For the bargain price of $1,000, the Yankees signed the young prodigy in 1949 and sent him to Independence, Kan., for his professional debut. A 26-homer, 136-RBI second season at Class D Joplin earned Mantle a rush trip to spring training with the Yankees, where he arrived amid almost-evangelical acclaim as the center field heir-apparent to Joe DiMaggio. When the Yankee players got their first look at the franchise's newest superstar, curiosity turned to shock.

"It was 18 years ago when a shy, naive teenager from Oklahoma arrived in the Yankee training camp," wrote veteran New York sportswriter Jim Ogle in a 1968

Young and naive, Mantle was not prepared for the intense New York spotlight when he joined the Yankees in 1951.

Everything about Mantle suggested power, from the determined eyes to the powerful arms that whipped his bat through pitches from either side of the plate.

edition of *The Sporting News*. "He wore a cheap straw hat and carried a four-buck cardboard suitcase, which must have brought howls from the sophisticated Yankees. They didn't laugh once they saw the young giant hit a baseball. ... He was destined to carry on the Yankees' superstar tradition which had begun in 1920 with Babe Ruth's arrival."

The Mantle aura was built around power—the long, towering drives that seemed to explode off his bat and beyond the boundaries of everyone's imagination. He didn't just hit the ball, he pounded it into oblivion. He did it with a Lou Gehrig-like force and Ruthian distance, a combination nobody had ever guessed possible.

He didn't just hit the ball, he pounded it into oblivion.

"I thought when I was playing with Ruth and Gehrig I was seeing all I was ever gonna see," said former Yankees catcher Bill Dickey, a coach with the team during Mantle's early years. "But this kid ... Ruth and Gehrig had power, but I've seen Mickey hit seven balls, seven so far ... well, I've never seen nothing like it."

Unfortunately, none of those monster mashes came in the early season of 1951, when oversold Yankee fans were expecting to see a combination of Ruth, Gehrig and DiMaggio rolled into one superstar package.

But Mantle, playing right field with DiMaggio in center, struggled out of the gate and excited fans quickly turned into jeering critics.

It was a shocking revelation for a 19-year-old, two years removed from high school and ill prepared for the transition from rural America to the bright lights of New York. As words like "yonder," "that there" and "shucks" captivated the New York media, his shy, withdrawn personality wilted in the city's intense spotlight. He was as far away from DiMaggio's poise and Ruth's articulate color as he was from Commerce, Okla.

Mantle was sent to Triple-A Kansas City to get back on track, returned to New York to complete a respectable rookie season and played in the first of 12 career World Series—a classic that set a career pattern for the

Spring training of 1951 was both a time for learning and impressing Yankee veterans with that special Mantle aura.

When Mantle tripped on a drain in Game 2 of the 1951 World Series, he suffered a knee injury that would plague him for the rest of his career.

blond-headed slugger. Chasing a Game 2 fly ball, Mantle stepped on a Yankee Stadium drain and tore tendons in his already delicate knee. Seldom would he run again without pain and never would he get through a whole season without missing playing time. And only months after his World Series mishap, young Mickey was stunned by the death of his 40-year-old father.

DiMaggio retired after the 1951 season and Mantle took over in center field. But first impressions can be difficult to overcome. The Mick spent the 1950s playing in DiMaggio's vast shadow and falling short in the eyes of New Yorkers, even though he emerged as one of the game's most dangerous hitters. In 1956 the young Oklahoman exploded into national prominence by winning a Triple Crown (.353, 52 home runs, 130 RBIs) and he followed that in 1957 with a .365 average, 34 homers and a second straight American League MVP award.

While unqualified popularity eluded Mantle, the microscope under which he operated did become more tolerable. Once lost in the bright New York glare, the Mick mixed comfortably in its nightlife, often accompanied by Yankee buddies Billy Martin and Whitey Ford. Once intimidated by the media and fans, he learned to work them to his advantage.

Mantle could be surly and brusque, but he also could charm quickly with his moon-faced smile and the innocence that literally oozed from his down-home personality. Having experienced the rigors of the Big Apple for nine years, he was much more understanding of its edgy intrusions when he was introduced to new teammate Roger Maris in the spring of 1960.

In 1956 the young Oklahoman exploded into national prominence...

◆

To put the unlikely home run pairing of Roger Maris and Mickey Mantle into perspective, consider this: Maris, with three so-so major league seasons under his belt, entered 1960 with 58 career home runs. Mantle, only three years older and with nine major league seasons on his superstar resume, already had hit 280. Maris had heard all about the Bambino, the humbling Yankee aura and the pressure of baseball under an intense, well-lit microscope. Mantle had lived it.

It didn't take long for Maris to experience the Babe Ruth mystique for himself—he shocked everybody by finishing his first New York July with a career-high 30 home runs. Suddenly the Fargo curiosity had become a midseason threat to the Bambino's single-season record of 60, and writers wanted to know how he felt about the possibility of breaking the most cherished mark in baseball.

Their careers overlapped in 1951 when the great Joe DiMaggio (left) passed his center field baton to the young and eager Mantle.

"I don't care about Ruth's record," became the familiar refrain from an overwhelmed Maris, who said he was only interested in driving in runs and helping the Yankees win games. As it turned out, Maris' early season home run barrage and the media reaction it sparked were merely appetizers for 1961. Maris injured his ribs in an August game against Washington while trying to break up a double play and his home run total fell off. He would finish the season with 39, one less than A.L. leader Mantle.

But Maris, who batted .283 and drove in a league-leading 112 runs, would top his teammate by an equally slim three-point margin in voting for the American League Most Valuable Player award. Thus was born the M&M legend, Mantle batting third in Stengel's explosive lineup and Maris protecting him from the fourth spot. That lineup helped the Yankees storm to their 11th A.L. pennant in 14 years and score 55 runs in a wild World Series against Pittsburgh. But the Pirates prevailed on Bill Mazeroski's shocking ninth-inning home run in Game 7 at Forbes Field.

Contrary to popular opinion, an intense Maris-Mantle rivalry was not born in that 1960 season. Just the opposite. Mantle appreciated what Maris brought to the Yankees lineup. And Maris, like everybody else, marveled at Mantle's power and special skills. What was born was a deep friendship, rooted by the similarities of their backgrounds and the intense spotlight they were destined to share.

In many ways, the M&M boys were kindred spirits:

◆ Fargo vs. Commerce. The transition from slow-paced, rural life to New York intensity was a culture shock for both. Mantle was totally unprepared for the media hornet's nest he was walking into when he made his debut as a 19-year-old prodigy and was quickly labeled an Oklahoma hillbilly. Maris understood that New York was a whole different world, but he still was not ready for the extremes of life in the big city—especially the demands of celebrity.

In many ways, the M&M boys were kindred spirits.

◆ Perceptions. Mantle was a blond-haired, moon-faced athletic specimen who could disarm fans with his shy smile and natural innocence. Maris also was impressive, a blond, crew-cut, jaw-jutting 6-footer who could have doubled as the Marine Corps poster boy. "Maris," Yankees coach Ralph Houk said in 1960, "is powerful all over."

◆ Personality. Both were quiet, withdrawn and serious, unlikely to speak until spoken to. Mantle went out of his way to accommodate fans and media during his early years but became brusque and moody later on. The no-nonsense Maris, whose patience was often tested by relentless New York writers, was portrayed as reticent and surly. "I was born surly and I intend to go on being that way," an amused Maris responded to the charge.

◆ Both were sons of miners, both were local legends and both married high school sweethearts. Both wives preferred to maintain households and raise their families away from the stifling spotlight of New York City. Pat Maris and her children lived in the Kansas City area while Mickey's wife Merlyn raised their family in Dallas.

There also were personality differences that separated the two Yankee sluggers.

An anatomy of two swings, Maris (left) in 1957 with the Indians and Mantle in 1950 with Joplin.

By the time Maris reached New York, Mantle was a man about town with expensive tastes and wardrobe to match.

◆ After getting acclimated to the big city, Mantle became a familiar face among the New York social crowd. Stories of his late-night drinking escapades with Martin and Ford, some of them obviously exaggerated, added to his Ruth-like mystique. Maris, on the other hand, preferred a quiet one or two-beer night at home, far from the maddening crowds.

◆ Maris had no interest in becoming a superstar. Mantle longed to fulfill his father's dream and live up to the lofty standard set by his predecessor and idol, DiMaggio.

◆ Maris was a practical, off-the-rack kind of guy who didn't worry a lot about perception. Baseball was his livelihood, a way to support his family. Mantle was a sharp dresser with designer tastes. His overall spending habits stood in stark contrast to Maris' thrifty lifestyle. Maris, after experimenting with life in Manhattan, ended up in an unpretentious Queens apartment with former Kansas City teammate Bob Cerv. Mantle, who in 1961 would share that apartment, lived for a long time at the St. Moritz hotel in an expensive suite and frequented expensive restaurants. Money was no object for Mantle, whether throwing team parties or picking up monster tabs at local establishments.

Mantle's overzealous spending and wild lifestyle might have stemmed in part from an unwavering belief that he would not live past age 40. His father, uncle and grandfather all had died young, victims of the Oklahoma zinc mines. Long after retirement, Mantle told friends that he would have lived life differently and taken better care of himself if he had known he was going to live so long.

When the 1960 season ended, Maris and Mantle already were linked in the minds of longtime New York fans, who suddenly were ready to embrace the Mick with fervor that previously had been reserved for Ruth, Gehrig and DiMaggio. That was the unwitting gift Maris delivered to his teammate. Roger, the interloper, ingratiated Mickey, the homegrown Yankee, to long unforgiving fans and guardians of that precious Yankee aura. Those feelings would intensify with each of the 115 home runs they would hit in the 1961 season.

'...I believe we have the best club in the league'

Whitey Ford, never a 20-game winner, was given a spring vote of confidence by new manager Ralph Houk (right, left photo)—a move that would pay off big time during the season. Roy Hamey (above) enjoyed his first spring training as the Yankees' general manager.

Spring of 1961 was all about renewal and hope. Newly inaugurated president John F. Kennedy was promising a bright and dynamic future for the burgeoning Baby Boomer generation, cultural breakthroughs were redefining the boundaries of art, music, education and just about every other facet of American life and Russian cosmonaut Yuri Gagarin was orbiting the earth in Vostok 1, touching off the incredible space race that would take man to the moon by the end of the decade.

A feeling of renewal also was sweeping through the Yankees' spring training camp in St. Petersburg, Fla.—the first in 12 years without Casey Stengel calling the managerial shots. The 70-year-old Stengel was gone after 12 incredible seasons (10 pennants, seven World Series titles), swept into retirement along with 65-year-old general manager George Weiss by the suddenly youth-conscious Yankees after their 1960 fall classic loss to the Pirates. Stengel had given way to 41-year-old Ralph Houk, a former Army major who had served as his coach since 1958, and Weiss had been replaced by Roy Hamey.

If nothing else, life without the Old Professor was calmer and gentler. While lacking the color and personality of the lovable Stengel, Houk provided a breath of fresh air for Yankee players, who were not always enamored with Casey's eccentric ways. Whereas Stengel could be distant and cold in his everyday dealings, prone to unexplained and sometimes-unusual actions, Houk was up front and easy to approach. Stengel was a control freak; Houk delegated authority. Stengel was a platoon manager who stuck with his veterans; Houk liked a set lineup and showed understanding and patience with his younger players. The Major's first big action was to demand more self-discipline from fun-

One of Houk's key spring moves was to endorse Tony Kubek (right, right photo) and Bobby Richardson as his '61 double play combination.

loving veterans Mickey Mantle and Whitey Ford, who were deemed incapable of handling leadership roles by Stengel.

"I believe that Mantle has arrived at that stage of his career when he can become the real leader of this ballclub on the field, the fellow the others look up to when the going gets rough," Houk told Dan Daniel in *The Sporting News*. "Players really like Mickey. He's popular in the clubhouse and around the league. Just think what he'd be like if he should really take hold of this ballclub the way I know he can."

Mantle shocked everybody by wandering into Houk's advance training camp and starting his season several days early. The 32-year-old Ford, never a 20-game winner, rejoiced when told he would start every fourth day, a departure from Stengel's belief that his 5-10, 181-pound body could not handle the strain of that workload.

As Yankees pitchers and catchers work out in St. Petersburg, Fla., Mickey Mantle (left) and Roger Maris discuss their 1961 prospects.

Houk quickly made it clear that he was running the show, whether instructing his young pitchers (above right) or barking out signals to coaches and players (below). Despite the new manager, despite the unsettled pitching staff, the Yankees were favored to win the American League pennant by *The Sporting News* (right).

Yankees vs. Dodgers in W.S., Scribes Say

By JOE COPPAGE

ST. LOUIS, Mo.

Major league writers, weighing each club's strong points against its weak spots just before the start of the new season, predict that the Yankees and Dodgers will meet in the World's Series next fall.

However, the scribes' opinion was far from unanimous. Balloting in the annual spring poll conducted by THE SPORTING NEWS, members of the Baseball Writers' Association of America scattered their first-place votes among no fewer than six clubs in the American League and five in the National League.

The Yankees were favored on 122 of the 234 votes cast in the A. L. balloting, a margin of slightly more than two to one, but the Dodgers, with 99, polled less than one-half of 232 votes cast for the top position in the N. L.

The Orioles, a surprise second-place club last year, were picked for the runner-up spot in the junior circuit, with 64 votes, while the White Sox, with 34, and the Indians, with 12, were pegged to repeat their third and fourth-place positions of 1960. The Tigers and Twins, with one top vote each, were rated fifth and sixth, followed by the Red Sox, Athletics, Angels and Senators.

* * *

Angels, Nats Pegged to Bring Up Rear

The writers gave the Angels and Senators, the new teams in the expanded A. L., little hope of overtaking the A's, who finished last in the 1960 eight-club circuit, but handed the Angels an edge over the Senators in the battle for ninth place.

In the N. L., the world's champion Pirates, with 58 votes, were ranked No. 2 behind the Dodgers, but Milwaukee, San Francisco and St. Louis also had their supporters. The Braves were the top choice of 38 scribes, while the Giants polled 22 votes and the Cardinals 15. The Reds, polling only five first-division ballots, were tabbed No. 6, while the Cubs and Phillies were assigned their 1960 seventh and eighth spots.

The Yankees were the only club which did not receive a second-division

IT IS TIME, SAYS YANKEE BRASS, FOR **MICKEY MANTLE** TO ASSUME THE ROLE OF INSPIRATIONAL LEADER...TO BE THE TAKE-CHARGE GUY... AND, AMONG OTHER THINGS, TO LEAD THE YANKS IN THEIR CHARGE FROM THE DUGOUT TO THEIR POSITIONS IN THE FIELD... EVEN AS JOE DI MAG IN DAYS OF YORE

Mick Gives Own Slant on 'Take-Charge' Role
By TIL FERDENZI

ST. PETERSBURG, Fla. — There is something take-charge about Mickey Mantle's views on the take-charge responsibility draped on his shoulders by Ralph Houk, new manager of the Yankees.

"You can't be a leader in anything just by popping off or yelling louder than everybody else," the Yankee center fielder said in a discussion of Houk's wish that Mantle be the leader of the Yankees this season. "There are other things mixed up in it. The other things,"

according to Mantle, "are what really make a leader—the kind Joe Di-Maggio was.

"People lead other people by their actions," Mickey said. "That's what I mean by the other things."

Mantle said he would "damn-well like to" be the leader Houk would

(CONTINUED ON PAGE 2, COL. 4)

Mantle's new role as a Yankee leader was greeted with interest by cartoonist Willard Mullin on the cover of *The Sporting News* (above). Spring training was calm and relaxing for Maris (right), who got in his cuts and enjoyed status as the reigning American League MVP.

"I have my own ideas how this job should be done and I'm not discarding Casey's system, either," said Houk, who pointed to a veteran lineup that included center fielder Mantle, right fielder Maris, first baseman Bill Skowron, second baseman Bobby Richardson, third baseman Clete Boyer and either Elston Howard or Yogi Berra behind the plate. "I have to sink or swim on my own. I believe we have the best club in the league and that our pitching is better than generally is supposed."

Among his deviations from script was a lineup that would open the season with Hector Lopez, a bench player under Stengel, in left field and Tony Kubek, a utility player in 1960, entrenched at shortstop. Houk made it clear from the beginning that youth would be served and spent much of the 1961 spring looking at such young pitchers as Rollie Sheldon, Bill Short, Jim Coates, Bill Stafford, Danny McDevitt and Luis Arroyo, his eventual closer. He also experimented freely with different lineup combinations, a risky strategy for a rookie manager.

Not surprisingly, many fans were nervous when the defending American League champions finished spring training with a 10-19 record. Early spring talk about Mantle making a run at Ruth's 34-year-old home run record had dissipated amid concerns that the Yankees might not be properly prepared to make their annual pennant run.

New York's M&M boys were just two more faces in the dugout when the stumbling Yanks closed down their final St. Petersburg spring training (they would move to Fort Lauderdale in 1962) and headed north to open the regular season against Minnesota on April 11 at Yankee Stadium.

WEEK 1		HOME RUN	ON BASE	INN.	SITE	PITCHER (THROWS)	GAME	PACE	RUTH'S PACE
APRIL 11		–	–	–	MINNESOTA (H)		1		
APRIL 12					OFF DAY				
APRIL 13					RAINOUT				
APRIL 14					OFF DAY				
APRIL 15		–	–	–	KANSAS CITY (H)		2		
APRIL 16					RAINOUT				
APRIL 17	MANTLE	1	1	1	KANSAS CITY (H)	WALKER (RH)	3	54	–
APRIL 18					RAINOUT				
APRIL 19					RAINOUT				

Despite the rain, the park and other things, Yankees weather a season-opening storm

WEEK

1

April 11-19

ickey Mantle drew first blood with a moonshot home run, a towering drive that bounced off the front facing of the upper tier at frigid Yankee Stadium. The first-inning, two-run shot off Kansas City righthander Jerry Walker in an April 17 game helped Whitey Ford post a 3-0 victory before 1,947 shivering New York fans.

Mantle's home run and Ford's shutout were the first real positive developments in a disjointed nine-day opening stretch in which the Yankees were limited to three games. Any notions of a fast start were washed away by a spring deluge that forced cancellation of five games and an early schedule that included two off days.

"The weather is raising plain hell with our pitchers," manager Ralph Houk moaned after an April 16 Sunday doubleheader against the A's was washed away. And, indeed, after nine days only Ford and Bob Turley had worked more than two innings—Ford starting in an opening-day 6-0 loss to Minnesota and Game 3 and Turley posting a Game 2 win over the A's.

It was difficult for Houk to get any read on his ballclub and difficult for either hitters or pitchers to garner any kind of momentum. Mantle had entered the third game without a hit in seven at-bats before getting a

home run and two singles.
Through Game 3,
Hector Lopez was
the only other
Yankee with an
extra-base hit (a third-
game double) and Roger
Maris was a humbling 1-for-9.

While Houk professed to be concerned only with the team's lack
of activity, he couldn't help but be
frustrated over the disparaging com-
mentary generated by a listless opening day loss. The former
Washington Senators, playing their first game as
the Minnesota

Ralph Houk, ready to open his first season as a major league manager, greets Twins manager Cookie Lavagetto (right) before the April 11 opener at Yankee Stadium. The opener brought together four of the game's premier power hitters—(left to right) Harmon Killebrew, Mickey Mantle, Jim Lemon and Maris.

The umpire signals out as Mantle crashes into Kansas City second baseman Jerry Lumpe while trying to break up a double play in the April 15 game at Yankee Stadium.

Twins, got a three-hit effort from righthander Pedro Ramos and home runs from Bob Allison and Reno Bertoia.

"It appears safe to say that never before in the history of the New York club as a pennant-winning organization has defeat in an opening game been productive of a bad reaction comparable to that which came of the Bombers' shutout setback by Minnesota on April 11—and for no good reason," Dan Daniel wrote in the April 26 issue of *The Sporting News*.

"The prophets of grief found an ally in the weather. ... The postponements gave the pessimists a lot of time to mull over the opening defeat, which in some places was magnified into a small catastrophe. ... All assumed the stand that Casey had been thrown out of his job and most wondered if the right man had been picked for the succession."

Yankees Record: 2-1   2nd   -1

WEEK 2		HOME RUN	ON BASE	INN.	OPPONENT (H) OR (A)	PITCHER (THROWS)	GAME	PACE	RUTH'S PACE
APRIL 20	MANTLE	2	1	1	LOS ANGELES (H)	GRBA (RH)	4	81	39
	MANTLE	3	2	5	LOS ANGELES (H)	GRBA (RH)	4	122	39
	–	–	–	–	LOS ANGELES (H)		5		
APRIL 21	MANTLE	4	1	3	BALTIMORE (A)	BARBER (LH)	6	108	26
APRIL 22		–	–	–	BALTIMORE (A)		7		
		–	–	–	BALTIMORE (A)		8		
APRIL 23	MANTLE	5	0	4	BALTIMORE (A)	ESTRADA (RH)	9	91	17
APRIL 24		–	–	–	DETROIT (A)		10		
APRIL 25					RAINOUT				
APRIL 26	MARIS	1	0	5	DETROIT (A)	FOYTACK (RH)	11	15	28
	MANTLE	6	1	8	DETROIT (A)	DONOHUE (RH)	11	89	28
	MANTLE	7	1	10	DETROIT (A)	AGUIRRE (LH)	11	104	28

The Mick shoots for the Moon as race for 60 gets off to fast start

WEEK

2

April 20-26

Roger Maris (9) and Yogi Berra (8) greet Mickey Mantle (right) after one of his two April 20 home runs against the Los Angeles Angels.

The Mickey Mantle show was playing to rave reviews, despite a stumbling six-game swing through Baltimore and Detroit that netted two wins, one tie and a lot of questions about the team's inconsistent start.

There was nothing inconsistent about Mantle, who belted seven home runs in eight official games after going hitless in his first seven at-bats of the season. Home runs 6 and 7 were marvelous theater, the stuff of which storybook endings are made. The 4,676 fans who made it to frosty Tiger Stadium April 26 were rewarded with one of the top slugging performances of the season.

With the Yankees trailing 11-9 in the top of the eighth inning, Mantle stepped to the plate with Tony Kubek on third base and drove a pitch from righthander Jim Donohue into the upper deck in right field, a prodigious shot that tied the game. Then, with Hector Lopez on base in the 10th, Mantle drove a pitch from lefthander Hank Aguirre into the upper deck in left, another impressive home run that gave the Yanks a 13-11 victory and snapped first-place Detroit's eight-game winning streak.

Writing in the April 26 issue of The Sporting News, Frederick G. Lieb offered this prediction going into the 1961 season:

"If any Ruth record will fall in the next five years, it is likely to be the one best known to fans, the Bambino's 60 homers in 1927. Two righthanded hitters, Jimmie Foxx and Hank Greenberg, gave Babe some real scares in the 1930s with 58 home runs each. Mickey Mantle, at the age of 24, came within eight of Babe's magic mark in 1956, but since then has not been close. ...

"Roger Maris, the Yankees' new star and most valuable 1960 A.L. player, was red hot for the first half of last season, but his history has been one of batting sprees, followed by dismal slumps and a general falling off in the second half of the season.

"Harmon Killebrew of the new Minnesota Twins made threatening motions toward Ruth's record in the spring and early summer of 1959, but slumped sharply in the season's second half and finished with 42. ... Helping sluggers Mantle, Maris, Killebrew and Roy Sievers even more than the additional eight games in 1961 are the weak pitching staffs of new Los Angeles and Washington clubs. ..."

Lost in the glow of Mantle's eighth career game with home runs from both sides of the plate was a solo homer by Roger Maris, his first of the season and only his seventh hit in 35 at-bats. Also overshadowed was an 18-hit outburst by the slumbering Yankees.

It was that kind of a week for Mantle, who hit his second and third home runs in the first game of a doubleheader against the expansion Los Angeles Angels and connected the next day in a 4-2 victory over the Orioles. With four home runs in six games, the inevitable "home run pace" talk got off to an early start.

"As Mantle did not hit his fourth homer last year until the Yanks' 24th game, he is now 18 games ahead of his 1960 pace," John Drebinger reported in the *New York Times*. "And he's eight games ahead of the pace set by Babe Ruth when he hit 60 homers in 1927 for the major league record."

The third member of the Yankees' early 1961 outfield was Hector Lopez (left), part of the Casey Stengel platoon in 1960. Lopez manned left field with Mantle in center and Maris in right.

Mantle was the April 26 hero, but he was joined in the home run circle by Maris (above left) and Tony Kubek (right). Mantle had seven home runs through that game, but he couldn't match the shocking total of eight posted by Los Angeles outfielder Wally Moon (below).

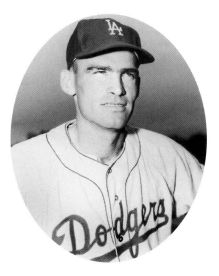

Dan Daniel, writing his "Over The Fence" column for *The Sporting News*, tried hard to resist the comparison temptation. "We who cover the Yankees also refer to the fact that Mickey Mantle is so many games and so many days ahead of the Babe's gait," he wrote. "And so it has gone from year to year, and so it will continue for many more years ... we of the press box are tempted to make silly comparisons." Daniel then went on to describe Ruth's record home run pace of 1927—in great detail.

Mantle added fuel to the fire when he hit his fifth homer in a 4-1 loss to the Orioles, setting the stage for his Detroit outburst.

Ironically, Mantle's home run total was not even high enough to lead the major leagues. Los Angeles Dodgers outfielder Wally Moon finished the week with eight home runs, a tribute more to his knack for hitting opposite-field fly balls at Memorial Coliseum than his slugging prowess. The lefthanded-hitting Moon was showing a proficiency for chipping balls over the 40-foot screen that served as a left field wall, only 251 feet from home plate.

"Many baseball people had gloomily forecast that hitters would make a joke out of this chummy extremity," TSN reported in its May 3 issue. "But no one anticipated it would be a lefthanded hitter."

Yankees Record: 6-4   T3rd   -2

WEEK 3		HOME RUN	ON BASE	INN.	OPPONENT (H) OR (A)	PITCHER (THROWS)	GAME	PACE	RUTH'S PACE
APRIL 27		–	–	–	CLEVELAND (H)		12		
APRIL 28					RAINOUT				
APRIL 29		–	–	–	CLEVELAND (H)		13		
APRIL 30		–	–	–	WASHINGTON (A)		14		
		–	–	–	WASHINGTON (A)		15		
MAY 1					RAINOUT				
MAY 2	MANTLE	8	3	10	MINNESOTA (A)	PASCUAL (RH)	16	82	58
MAY 3	MARIS	2	2	7	MINNESOTA (A)	RAMOS (RH)	17	19	55

WEEK

3

April 27 - May 3

Mantle's bat keeps blazing and slow-starting Yankees catch fire

As the blazing bat of Mickey Mantle continued to wreak havoc on American League pitchers, the Yankee machine began rolling toward its usual October destiny. Five wins in six games served notice that Ralph Houk's first team was seriously in pursuit of the franchise's 26th pennant and Mantle's fast start was raising expectations that something special was in the air.

"The way he is hitting and the way he is fielding," Houk told TSN correspondent Joe King, "I don't think he has to do or say more to be this team's leader."

Mantle's seventh-inning triple drove home the winning run in a 4-3 win over Cleveland at Yankee Stadium and then he saved that victory with a lunging, skidding catch of a ninth-inning drive by Bubba Phillips. Four days later, Mantle drove a 10th-inning pitch from Minnesota's Camilo Pascual 430 feet over the center field fence at Metropolitan Stadium for a game-deciding grand slam—his eighth home run of the season.

By the time the Yankees had completed their three-game Minnesota sweep, Mantle owned a 16-game hitting streak, starting pitchers Whitey Ford, Bob Turley and Art Ditmar were settling into a winning routine and Roger Maris was showing signs of shaking his season-opening slump. Game 2 at Minnesota, a 7-3 Yankees victory, was fueled by Maris' three-run shot off Twins righthander Pedro Ramos.

Mickey Mantle (lower photo, right) opened the season with bat blazing while outfield partner Roger Maris struggled out of the gate. One of the season's top power displays was put on April 30 when San Francisco's Willie Mays (above) hit four home runs in a game against Milwaukee.

While Mantle's early assault was drawing plenty of attention, it couldn't draw the spotlight away from an even more remarkable performance by Willie Mays. The San Francisco center fielder, enjoying "the greatest day of my career," muscled up to hit four homers and drive in eight runs during the Giants' 14-4 win at Milwaukee, becoming only the ninth player in baseball history to perform that feat.

Mays, who battled fellow center fielder Mantle for the hearts of New York fans when the Giants were located there, connected in the first, third, sixth and eighth innings and was kneeling in the on-deck circle when teammate Jim Davenport grounded out to end the game.

Yankees Record: 11-5 T1st —

WEEK 4		HOME RUN	ON BASE	INN.	OPPONENT (H) OR (A)	PITCHER (THROWS)	GAME	PACE	RUTH'S PACE
MAY 4	MANTLE	9	0	6	MINNESOTA (A)	SADOWSKI (RH)	18	82	52
MAY 5		–	–	–	LOS ANGELES (A)		19		
MAY 6	MARIS	3	0	5	LOS ANGELES (A)	GRBA (RH)	20	24	47
MAY 7		–	–	–	LOS ANGELES (A)		21		
MAY 8					OFF DAY				
MAY 9		–	–	–	KANSAS CITY (A)		22		
MAY 10		–	–	–	KANSAS CITY (A)		23		

Devilish Angels cool off Mantle, deflate Yankees' ego

WEEK

4

May 4-10

By the end of Week 4, Roger Maris (above right) was showing signs of emerging from his early season funk. An important player was added to the Yankees bench when pitcher Ryne Duren (center) was traded late in the week to Los Angeles for Bob Cerv (below).

A funny thing happened to the Yankees on their way to first place. As rumors circulated that Casey Stengel would become manager of the expansion New York Mets in 1962, the Bronx Bombers crash landed in Los Angeles, struggled to maintain altitude in Kansas City and limped home to face the American League-leading Detroit Tigers with their top gun firing blanks.

The team's first regular-season trip to the West Coast was a disappointment. The Yankees, who had won seven of eight games and appeared ready to challenge the Tigers, edged the expansion Angels, 5-4, as third baseman Clete Boyer homered and drove in three runs in the series opener. But that's as good as it got against the A.L. newcomers, who rose up to post consecutive 5-3 wins.

Not only did the Angels dent the Yankees' well-exposed ego, they brought Mantle back to earth with a thud. The A.L. home run (9) and RBI (24) leader went hitless in 11 official at-bats against the Angels and struck out three times in the series finale, including once with runners on second and third.

When the Yankees and ace Whitey Ford fell again in a 5-4 series-opening loss at Kansas City, there was reason for concern. But the Yanks salvaged the second game 9-7 and Mantle ended his 18-at-bat hitless streak with an eighth-inning single.

Two positives came out of Los Angeles. Maris, slowly regaining his 1960 form, hit career home run No. 100 in the second-game loss to the Angels. And the Yankees pulled the trigger on a five-player trade that brought power-hitting outfielder Bob Cerv back to the Yankees for a third time.

Cerv, who was acquired along with righthanded reliever Tex Clevenger for outfielder Leroy Thomas and pitchers Ryne Duren and Johnny James, was important because of the chemistry he added to the M&M mix. Maris and Cerv, friends from their 1958-59 seasons in Kansas City, would become New York roommates and Mantle soon would join them in their Queens apartment.

Yankees Record: 14-8   2nd   -3

WEEK 5		HOME RUN	ON BASE	INN.	OPPONENT (H) OR (A)	PITCHER (THROWS)	GAME	PACE	RUTH'S PACE
MAY 11					OFF DAY				
MAY 12		–	–	–	DETROIT (H)		24		
MAY 13		–	–	–	DETROIT (H)		25		
MAY 14		–	–	–	DETROIT (H)		26		
		–	–	–	DETROIT (H)		27		
MAY 15					OFF DAY				
MAY 16	MANTLE	10	0	6	WASHINGTON (H)	WOODESHICK (LH)	28	58	44
MAY 17	MARIS	4	1	8	WASHINGTON (H)	BURNSIDE (LH)	29	22	48

'Mantle must be Mantle or the lads will view the World's Series on TV in October'

◆
WEEK

5

May 11-17

As weeks go, this one was not a Yankee masterpiece. But their two wins in six games were strategically placed and they escaped their pratfall without serious damage.

While regulars Roger Maris, Moose Skowron, Bobby Richardson, Yogi Berra and Hector Lopez continued to battle their way out of slumps and Mickey Mantle was hobbled by a pulled calf muscle, manager Ralph Houk juggled his pitching staff and waited for the inevitable offensive explosion. His patience, like his unyielding optimism, was being tested daily.

"The Yankees can be pegged this simply—Mantle must be Mantle or the lads will view the World's Series on TV in October," Joe King warned in *The Sporting News*. "There are other vaunted bats on the Yankees, but it seems that the Switcher must lead and then they follow."

An important early season showdown with first-place Detroit supported that statement. It started ominously at Yankee Stadium when right-hander Frank Lary, who had built a career around his ability to beat the Yankees with his arm, drilled a ninth-inning home run off Jim Coates to give the Tigers a 4-3 victory. Game 2 also went to the Tigers, 8-3, as Rocky Colavito hit two home runs.

The classic power swing of Mickey Mantle (above) produced 10 home runs in an early season blitz that kept the Yankees in touch with the equally hot Detroit Tigers. During a mid-May trip to Yankee Stadium, Yankees Roger Maris (left, right photo) and Mantle (right) posed with Detroit power men Rocky Colavito (center left) and Norm Cash (center right).

But just when it appeared the Tigers might bury the Yankees in a deep hole, the Bombers rebounded for a 5-4 (11 innings) and 8-6 doubleheader sweep that cut their deficit to 2½ games. To no one's surprise, the double victory was keyed by the hitting of Mantle, who limped his way to five hits in eight at-bats while scoring five runs.

The Yankee longball parade, expected to march through the American League like General Sherman through Atlanta, was way off schedule through games of May 17. The Yanks had played 28 times (16-12) and hit 29 home runs—14 combined by their Big Two of Maris and Mantle. The Mick's 10th home run was one of two hits by the Yankees in a 3-2 May 16 loss to Washington's Hal Woodeshick and Maris' fourth came the next day off lefty Pete Burnside in an 8-7 loss to the Senators.

Yankees Record: 16-12   2nd   -5

WEEK 6		HOME RUN	ON BASE	INN.	OPPONENT (H) OR (A)	PITCHER (THROWS)	GAME	PACE	RUTH'S PACE
MAY 18					OFF DAY				
MAY 19	MARIS	5	1	1	CLEVELAND (A)	J. PERRY (RH)	30	27	47
MAY 20	MARIS	6	0	3	CLEVELAND (A)	BELL (RH)	31	32	45
MAY 21	MARIS	7	0	1	BALTIMORE (H)	ESTRADA (RH)	32	36	44
		–	–	–	BALTIMORE (H)		33		
MAY 22		–	–	–	BALTIMORE (H)		34		
MAY 23					OFF DAY				
MAY 24	MARIS	8	1	4	BOSTON (H)	CONLEY (RH)	35	37	49

Sudden home run burst lifts Maris out of his early season funk

◆

WEEK

6

May 18-24

Roger Maris (right), finally swinging the bat with 1960-like efficiency, hit home runs in four consecutive games and took some of the sting out of Mickey Mantle's sudden slump.

I t was a master stroke, the same one that had lifted Roger Maris to MVP heights in 1960. Missing through the first five weeks of the season, it suddenly returned in mid-May to set the stage for the greatest single-season home run duel in baseball history.

After connecting for his fourth home run in the Week 5-ending loss to Washington, Maris hit a two-run shot in his next game off Cleveland's Jim Perry, a solo blast a day later off Cleveland's Gary Bell and another bases-empty blow off Baltimore righthander Chuck Estrada in the opener of a doubleheader.

Maris failed to stretch his home run-hitting streak to five games, but he did deliver a two-run shot May 24 against Boston's Gene Conley and edged closer to an American League leaders list that included Baltimore's Jim Gentile (12), Minnesota's Harmon Killebrew (11), Detroit's Rocky Colavito (11), teammate Mickey Mantle (10), Chicago's Roy Sievers and Los Angeles' Leon Wagner (9).

Maris' sudden revival came at a perfect time for the Yankees, who still struggled through a 3-3 week that ended with the team in third place, six games behind Detroit and a game and a half behind Cleveland. The Maris home runs were the only highlights of a two-game Cleveland sweep that ended the Indians' 11-game losing streak to the Yankees.

Not all of Maris' Week 6 was
spent doing the home run trot,
as evidenced by the double play
grounder he beat out May 21 (above)
against Baltimore. The May 22 game
became a source of controversy
when Maris, who had made a
surprise visit to the eye doctor
earlier in the day, had to be removed
from the lineup after a bad reaction
to eye drops. Maris (right) examines
his irritated eyes in the Yankees
clubhouse.

"The hitting is sputtery, but anybody will agree that when Mickey
Mantle does hit, he is hard to beat," Joe King reported in his weekly
TSN notes. "Roger Maris and Bill Skowron also can carry the team at
tops. However, Mantle has not been murderously inclined towards
the pitched ball over any long period since his early flurry of homers.
Houk had to bench Skowron May 22 after the Moose was 0-for-10 in
three games.

"The Moose slumped just when Maris indicated he was coming to life
in his MVP form of last season, with four homers in four successive
games into the Baltimore opener on May 21. If Maris has a first half
such as he enjoyed in '60, the team can wait on Mantle and Skowron
to recharge their batteries."

The week was not without a Yankee controversy—and this one, ironically, focused squarely on Maris. The May 22 game against Baltimore at
Yankee Stadium started normally enough with Maris stationed in right
field, but he was removed suddenly after a half inning, causing more
than a minor stir in the press box.

"Roger used some eye drops just before the game and he apparently was allergic to them," Houk explained to curious writers after Clete Boyer's three-run homer had keyed an 8-2 Yankees' victory. "It was just a temporary, minor thing. ..."

Temporary yes. Minor no. When prodded, Houk admitted that he was extremely upset that Maris had visited his eye doctor on the day of a game—right in the midst of his most productive stretch of the season. Maris, it turned out later, had been ordered to visit the doctor by concerned Yankees management, without Houk's knowledge.

After a Yankees' off day, everything settled down when Maris' homer and Tony Kubek's ninth-inning single gave the Yanks a 3-2 win over Boston.

Yankees Record: 19-15   3rd   -6

WEEK 7		HOME RUN	ON BASE	INN.	OPPONENT (H) OR (A)	PITCHER (THROWS)	GAME	PACE	RUTH'S PACE
MAY 25		–	–	–	BOSTON (H)		36		
MAY 26					RAINOUT				
MAY 27					RAINOUT				
MAY 28		–	–	–	CHICAGO (H)		37		
	MARIS	9	1	2	CHICAGO (H)	McLISH (RH)	38	39	49
MAY 29	MANTLE	11	0	7	BOSTON (A)	DeLOCK (RH)	39	46	52
MAY 30	MANTLE	12	2	1	BOSTON (A)	CONLEY (RH)	40	49	50
	MARIS	10	0	3	BOSTON (A)	CONLEY (RH)	40	41	50
	MARIS	11	2	8	BOSTON (A)	FORNIELES (RH)	40	45	50
	MANTLE	13	0	8	BOSTON (A)	FORNIELES (RH)	40	53	50
MAY 31	MARIS	12	0	3	BOSTON (A)	MUFFETT (RH)	41	48	53
	MANTLE	14	1	4	BOSTON (A)	MUFFETT (RH)	41	56	53

Maris, Mantle, Yankees flex muscles as annual June push begins

WEEK

7

May 25-31

Binge week started quietly enough when two-run homers by Tony Kubek and Johnny Blanchard keyed a 6-4 victory over Boston at Yankee Stadium. It ended five games later when, fittingly, Roger Maris and Mickey Mantle connected during a 7-6 win over the Red Sox at Fenway Park.

From May 25 through 31, the suddenly revived Bombers gave New York fans a heaping helping of what they had expected all along—home runs, enough to finally fulfill even the preseason fantasies of manager Ralph Houk. Maris (four) and Mantle (four), continuing their impressive first-half assault on American League pitchers, accounted for half of the 16 Yankee long balls in a six-game stretch that sent familiar rumbles through baseball.

"Almost every year, June is the month the Yankees make their big push to establish themselves strongly in contention for still another pennant," warned Joe King in the June 7 issue of *The Sporting News*. "It looks as if it will be that way under Ralph Houk, as it was under Casey Stengel."

The Yankees bomb squad exploded for seven home runs in a May 30 win at Boston. Yogi Berra (right) hit only one while (left to right) Moose Skowron, Roger Maris and Mickey Mantle all connected twice.

The biggest rumble could be felt May 30, after the Yankees unloaded seven home runs—one short of the A.L. record—in a 12-3 onslaught at Boston. With Maris, Mantle and Moose Skowron connecting twice and Yogi Berra once, the Yankees raked righthanders Gene Conley, Dave Hillman and Mike Fornieles with Maris and Mantle combining for five hits and eight RBIs.

When the M&M boys both homered again the next day at Boston, they closed out a streaky first six weeks filled with slumps, hitting rampages and team ups and downs.

"Roger Maris, who had a tough fight to make .200 in the first five weeks, went on a rampage the last half of May," King wrote in TSN. "On May 16, he had three homers. On May 31, he had 12. Roger hit nine in 12 games. Mickey Mantle, after a long slump, regained his magic power as May closed. He hit four homers in three games in Boston, May 29-31." Mantle led the A.L. with 14 home runs as May closed while Maris stood at 12, behind Baltimore's Jim Gentile (13) and

REG. U. S. PAT. OFF.

VOLUME 151, NUMBER 20   ST. LOUIS, JUNE 7, 1961   PRICE: TWENTY-FIVE CENTS

GOOD OLD DAYS OVER, YANKEES PLUNGE INTO BONUS BINGE

Mantle (above left) and manager Ralph Houk (right) discuss hitting with new Yankees bonus baby Jake Gibbs (center), whose signing was greeted with headline fascination by the media. The sight of Mantle batting and Maris leading off first (right photo) was familiar in 1961, as was news of Mantle's never-ending injury problems.

Taped-Up Mick Busts Loose on Home-Run Binge

Crippled Mantle Hits Four in Three Games, Leads in Onslaught Against Bosox

By JOE KING
BOSTON, Mass.

Ralph Houk never knows when Mickey Mantle is going to bust loose or break down. A series of injuries to his underpinning afflicted the switcher in late May.

When Mickey withdrew from **Mickey Mantle** the double-header with the White Sox in New York, May 27, Manager Houk felt that his star might be laid up some time.

Then — boom. With yards of tape supporting his ailing right leg, Mickey slammed a homer in Fenway Park off Ike Delock, May 29, in the 2 to 1 defeat for Whitey Ford.

Mantle cracked two more, May 30, in a seven-homer assault against Boston and hit his fourth the next day.

The seven-homer onslaught, one shy of the record set by the '39 Bombers

tied with Detroit's Rocky Colavito (12) and Minnesota's Harmon Killebrew. The 23-17 Yankees were hovering in third place behind Detroit and Cleveland, ready to pounce.

Lost in the glare of the home run spotlight were the early week headlines announcing the signing of third baseman Jake Gibbs for an almost incomprehensible bonus that totaled somewhere between $100,000 and $125,000. The former Mississippi All-American quarterback joined the Yankees for a two-week training stint that would eventually result in his assignment to Richmond.

Yankees Record: 23-17 3rd -3½

WEEK 8		HOME RUN	ON BASE	INN.	OPPONENT (H) OR (A)	PITCHER (THROWS)	GAME	PACE	RUTH'S PACE
JUNE 1		–	–	–	BOSTON (A)		42		
JUNE 2	MARIS	13	2	3	CHICAGO (A)	McLISH (RH)	43	49	58
JUNE 3	MARIS	14	2	8	CHICAGO (A)	SHAW (RH)	44	52	56
JUNE 4	MARIS	15	0	3	CHICAGO (A)	KEMMERER (RH)	45	54	55
JUNE 5	MANTLE	15	2	8	MINNESOTA (H)	MOORE (RH)	46	53	54
		–	–	–	MINNESOTA (H)		47		
JUNE 6	MARIS	16	2	6	MINNESOTA (H)	PALMQUIST (RH)	48	54	58
JUNE 7	MARIS	17	2	3	MINNESOTA (H)	RAMOS (RH)	49	57	57

Yankees enjoy power surge as Maris blitzes into league lead

WEEK

8

June 1-7

A three-paragraph item in the June 14 issue of *The Sporting News* echoed the skepticism of baseball fans from coast to coast. "Mysterious Roger Maris," it began and then proceeded to recount the Jekyll-Hyde nature of the Yankee right fielder's streaky baseball career.

The revelation was not lost on hardened New Yorkers, who had viewed fruitless assaults on Babe Ruth's single-season home run record with a combination of amusement and disdain for 34 years. That included the 1960 half-season run of Yankees newcomer Maris, who hit 30 homers by July 20 before sliding into a second-half funk.

So it didn't exactly set off fireworks when Maris, who had struggled mightily through May 16, put together a home run blitz that would have pleased even the immortal Bambino. Maris hit his fourth homer of the season on May 17 and then hit one in each of the next three games. Through games of June 7, the Maris blitz had reached 14 homers in 21 games and he stood atop the A.L. leaderboard with 17, two ahead of teammate Mantle and Detroit's Rocky Colavito.

But of more immediate interest to New York baseball writers was the impressive power surge by the suddenly rampaging Yankees. "With a spectacular surge of power, the Yankees swept to a record a day in

Maris watches the flight of his 17th home run, a tremendous drive that reached the right field upper deck at Yankee Stadium. Also watching is Minnesota catcher Hal Naragon.

marathon homer hitting beginning on June 2 in Chicago," Joe King wrote in TSN.

During that 6-2 win at Chicago, Yogi Berra homered twice and Maris hit one to give the Yankees 23 home runs in 10 consecutive games, an A.L. record. After a June 5 doubleheader sweep of Minnesota, the record had risen to 28 in 14 games—10 of which were hit by Maris.

While Maris' home run and RBI (43) totals were swelling, Mantle was struggling through a one-homer week in which his average fell more than 10 points. No problem.

With Maris leading the charge and teammates Berra, Bill Skowron and Tony Kubek adding occasional muscle, the Yankees won six times in eight games. Lost in the long-ball shadow was the pitching of Whitey Ford, who won twice and raised his record to 8-2.

Yankees Record: 29-19 3rd -3

WEEK 9		HOME RUN	ON BASE	INN.	OPPONENT (H) OR (A)	PITCHER (THROWS)	GAME	PACE	RUTH'S PACE
JUNE 8		–	–	–	KANSAS CITY (H)		50		
		–	–	–	KANSAS CITY (H)		51		
JUNE 9	MANTLE	16	2	3	KANSAS CITY (H)	HERBERT (RH)	52	50	60
	MARIS	18	1	7	KANSAS CITY (H)	HERBERT (RH)	52	56	60
JUNE 10	MANTLE	17	0	8	KANSAS CITY (H)	KUNKEL (RH)	53	52	61
JUNE 11		–	–	–	LOS ANGELES (H)		54		
	MANTLE	18	2	1	LOS ANGELES (H)	GRBA (RH)	55	53	62
	MARIS	19	0	3	LOS ANGELES (H)	GRBA (RH)	55	56	62
	MARIS	20	0	7	LOS ANGELES (H)	JAMES (RH)	55	59	62
JUNE 12		–	–	–	LOS ANGELES (H)		56		
JUNE 13	MARIS	21	0	6	CLEVELAND (A)	J. PERRY (RH)	57	60	60
JUNE 14	MARIS	22	1	4	CLEVELAND (A)	BELL (RH)	58	62	59

Something special's in the air as home run derby heats up

WEEK

9

June 8-14

It was a preview, a prelude to the most spectacular home run show in baseball history.

Mickey Mantle, master of the long, towering, upper-deck homer, hit an impressive three-run shot off Los Angeles Angels righthander Eli Grba in the first inning of the second game of a June 11 doubleheader sweep at Yankee Stadium. Not only did the blow give Rollie Sheldon a nice cushion in pursuit of his third victory, it tied Mantle for the A.L. home run lead with 18. Briefly.

Roger Maris answered that challenge two innings later with a solo shot off Grba, his 19th, and he struck again in the seventh off Johnny James with the bases empty—a simple, everyday Maris-type drive into the right field stands that lifted his total to 20.

It was quickly becoming apparent something special was taking shape. Mantle had touched off whispers about Babe Ruth and a home run pace with his early season rampage, but they had died away. Now, in tandem, New York's M&M boys were pounding their way into the

The 1961 season was not all about Roger Maris and Mickey Mantle home runs. Maris (above) showed his defensive side with a homer-robbing catch of a ball hit by Los Angeles' Ken Hunt before tumbling into the Yankee Stadium stands in a June 11 game. Maris (right) could not quite reach the ball hit by A's pitcher Joe Nuxhall the night before.

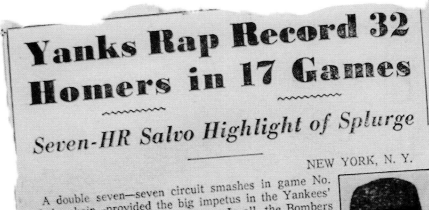

Yanks Rap Record 32 Homers in 17 Games

Seven-HR Salvo Highlight of Splurge

NEW YORK, N. Y.

Roger Maris

A double seven—seven circuit smashes in game No. 7 of the skein—provided the big impetus in the Yankees' recent record-smashing homer spree. In all, the Bombers walloped 32 round-trippers in a 17-game stretch for an American League record before Kansas City's Jim Archer applied the brakes to the four-bagger splurge in the second half of a twin-bill, June 8.

The homer skein began innocently enough. In 33 games through May 21, the Yankees had hit just 34 circuit smashes. The next evening, Clete Boyer rapped a four-master against Baltimore to launch the binge. In the first six games of the streak, the Yankees hit only nine homers, but then came the big seven-homer explosion at Boston on Memorial Day. The seven-gun salute marked the twenty-first time in major league history that one club has hit seven or more in a game, according to Leonard Gettelson, compiler of "One for the Book." The record for most four-baggers by a team in a contest is eight.

While the Yankees broke the former A. L. 17-game mark of 29 set by the 1941 Bombers, they fell two short of the N. L. record for that span, established by Cincinnati in 1956.

The '41 Bombers ran their homer streak to 25 consecutive games—another record—before finally being stopped.

Altogether, eight players contributed to the Yankees' latest skein. Roger Maris accounted for ten of the 32 clouts, while Yogi Berra had six, Bill Skowron and Mickey Mantle five each; John Blanchard and Tony Kubek two apiece, and Boyer and Bob Cerv one each.

A breakdown of the Yankees' streak, as well as a list of clubs with seven or eight homers in a game as compiled by Gettelson, follow:

Date—Opponent—Homers	Date—Opponent—Homers
5-22—Baltimore....Boyer	6-1—Boston.............Skowron 2
5-24—Boston...........Maris	6-2—Chicago..........Berra 2, Maris
5-25—Boston...........Blanchard, Kubek	6-3—Chicago..........Maris
5-28—Chicago.........Cerv, Berra, S...	6-4—Chicago.........Maris
	...Mantle

The Yankees' home run-hitting exploits, not just those of Maris and Mantle, caught the attention of the baseball world in early 1961. But homers were not the only area of expertise exhibited by the M&M boys. With Maris in right field and Mantle in center (right photo), few balls fell untouched into those areas of the field.

national spotlight. Word was spreading about the long-ball exploits of Maris, Mantle and Detroit sluggers Norm Cash and Rocky Colavito, attracting crowds to American League ballparks in ever-increasing multitudes.

"I just hope the boys can continue to hit like this," gushed Yankees manager Ralph Houk. "I get to watch them do it for free."

As the Maris-Mantle pace speeded up, so did Houk's pennant express. The Yankees boss, having settled on a lineup with Maris batting third and Mantle fourth, was getting plenty of offensive mileage from his peripheral cast. Lefthander Bud Daley had been acquired from Kansas City for Art Ditmar, filling a rotation void. Ace Whitey Ford was cruising along with a 10-2 record.

Two of Ford's victories came in Week 9 as the Yankees won seven of nine games and completed a 12-of-14 streak to pull within one game of the first-place Indians and Tigers. Mantle hit his 17th home run in Ford's 5-3 win over Kansas City and Maris hit No. 22 (his fifth of the week) in an 11-5 victory over Cleveland. Amazingly, either Mantle or Maris had homered in eight of Ford's 10 wins.

When the dust had cleared, Maris sat atop the A.L. home run leaderboard with 22, three ahead of Cash and four in front of Mantle.

Yankees Record: 36-21   3rd   -1

WEEK 10		HOME RUN	ON BASE	INN.	OPPONENT (H) OR (A)	PITCHER (THROWS)	GAME	PACE	RUTH'S PACE
JUNE 15	MANTLE	19	0	7	CLEVELAND (A)	GRANT (RH)	59	52	58
JUNE 16		–	–	–	DETROIT (A)		60		
JUNE 17	MARIS	23	0	4	DETROIT (A)	MOSSI (LH)	61	61	61
	MANTLE	20	2	9	DETROIT (A)	FOYTACK (RH)	61	53	61
JUNE 18	MARIS	24	1	8	DETROIT (A)	CASALE (RH)	62	63	60
JUNE 19	MARIS	25	0	9	KANSAS CITY (A)	ARCHER (LH)	63	65	59
JUNE 20	MARIS	26	0	1	KANSAS CITY (A)	NUXHALL (LH)	64	66	58
JUNE 21	MANTLE	21	2	1	KANSAS CITY (A)	SHAW (RH)	65	53	57
	MANTLE	22	1	7	KANSAS CITY (A)	SHAW (RH)	65	55	57

A little home cooking keeps Maris on homer fast track

♦
WEEK
10

June 15-21

For Roger Maris, it was a homecoming to remember, a time for family, friends and a few more notches in his home run bat. For Mickey Mantle, it was just another city, another pitching staff to terrorize and another opportunity to showcase one of the most explosive swings in baseball history.

"Kansas City here I come" took on new meaning June 19 when the Yankees' home run roadshow made a four-day Missouri stop in the middle of a grueling 16-game trip. Heading the New York cast were adopted son Maris, the major league home run leader who called Kansas City home, and the legendary Mantle, who had spent part of a minor league season there in 1951.

Fans hoping to experience the Maris home run magic that had been sweeping over baseball were not disappointed—and they got a large dose of Mantle to boot. Maris connected two times in the first three games (Nos. 25 and 26) and Mantle added two of the longest balls ever hit at Kansas City's Municipal Stadium, Nos. 21 and 22.

"When Roger Maris clouted his 26th homer off veteran Joe Nuxhall (in Kansas City) June 20, it became time to sit up and take notice of the amazing statistics being recorded by the Yankee right fielder and MVP of 1960," Joe King wrote in *The Sporting News*. "After hitting only

A trip to Kansas City means a brief respite from baseball for Roger Maris, who maintains his permanent home in nearby Raytown. Maris (above) plays with the youngest of his four children as wife Pat looks on in the living room of their house.

three homers in the first 27 Bomber decisions, Maris caught fire May 17 and accounted for 23 four-baggers in the next 36 games."

For Maris, it was a relaxing four days with wife Pat and his four children at their Raytown home. Home runs in the first two games off lefties Jim Archer and Nuxhall were icing on the cake. But for pure showmanship, Mantle was hard to beat.

The Mick drove in all the Yankee runs in Bud Daley's first win for New York, a 5-3 decision over A's righthander Bob Shaw in the third game of the series. The first of two home runs was a towering shot that bounced off the huge scoreboard positioned well beyond the right-center field fence. The second was a moonshot that cleared both the regular right field fence and the 40-foot outer fence, bouncing to freedom on Brooklyn Avenue, 490-plus feet from home plate. It was only the fourth ball to clear the outer wall—the second by Mantle.

Despite the heavy artillery that included three home runs by Moose Skowron and two by Johnny Blanchard, the Yankees stumbled through a 4-3 Week 10 that left them in second place, one game behind the Tigers. Two Maris homers and one by Mantle could not keep New York

TSNarchives

This editorial ran in the July 28 issue of The Sporting News:

Some time between now and the All-Star Game, the American League should give some thought to the present season which, to put it mildly, has been a unique one for the circuit.

It was expected to be because of the expanison. There was some concern that hard-earned records might be easily fractured in 1961.

This concern is now heightened. With less than half the season completed, some players individually and some clubs collectively are within sight of some awesome slugging records.

The lengthened season is partially responsible for this. A more immediate factor, however, is the caliber of some of the talent. Without taking anything away from any of the sluggers, it is evident that they are fattening up against hurlers who might otherwise be in the minor leagues.

This same factor accounts for some of the wild games, where six, seven and eight-run innings are almost commonplace. When expansion levels off, this matter will take care of itself, but the American League must consider now whether it is to accept this year's records as bona fide.

A major chunk of the June 28 cover of *The Sporting News* (right) was devoted to the slugging tandem of Mantle and Maris (left), who already were being projected as a threat to the 1927 teammate home run record of Babe Ruth and Lou Gehrig. TSN also editorialized (above) on the impact all 1961 sluggers might have on baseball's record book.

from losing two of three in a first-place battle at Detroit, but the Yanks came back strong in Kansas City with Maris continuing his blistering pace.

"Maris actually was ahead of Ruth's (1927 home run) pace with his 26th in his 64th game," King duly reported. "The Babe notched No. 26 in his 73rd game."

Yankees Record: 40-24 2nd -1

WEEK 11		HOME RUN	ON BASE	INN.	OPPONENT (H) OR (A)	PITCHER (THROWS)	GAME	PACE	RUTH'S PACE
JUNE 22	MARIS	27	1	2	KANSAS CITY (A)	BASS (RH)	66	67	56
JUNE 23		–	–	–	MINNESOTA (A)		67		
JUNE 24		–	–	–	MINNESOTA (A)		68		
JUNE 25		–	–	–	MINNESOTA (A)		69		
JUNE 26	MANTLE	23	0	2	LOS ANGELES (A)	McBRIDE (RH)	70	54	55
JUNE 27		–	–	–	LOS ANGELES (A)		71		
JUNE 28	MANTLE	24	1	9	LOS ANGELES (A)	DUREN (RH)	72	54	54

'I hope you believe me when I say I never give Babe Ruth a thought'

WEEK

11

June 22-28

Roger Maris' home run bat (right) might have cooled off, but Babe Ruth's single-season record became a hot topic among curious sports reporters.

Just as the blistering home run pace cooled dramatically, interest began to heat up. And with that interest came inevitable questions about Babe Ruth and his 60-home run legacy.

"I'll bet you lie awake at night thinking about how you're going to break Babe Ruth's record," one New York writer asked Roger Maris after he had hit his 27th home run in the series finale at Kansas City. Maris' face turned red and the hairs on his crew-cut head almost bristled.

"I want you all to know one thing," he said, pointing at his questioner. "I hope you believe me when I say I never give Babe Ruth a thought. Not now or ever. I do not think about his record. I'm just surprised I'm able to hit this many. Thankful, too."

Maris' major league-leading 27th homer came off A's righthander Norm Bass, a three-run shot that helped Whitey Ford post his 12th victory in 14 decisions. It was his 15th in June, three short of the big-league record for one month, and his 24th in 38 games. But suddenly, like someone turning off the home run faucet, they stopped coming.

A three-game swing through Minnesota resulted in two Yankee wins, but no home runs for either Maris or outfield partner Mickey Mantle. Maris came up dry in a three-game set at Los Angeles while Mantle

As the halfway point of the season approached, it was becoming increasingly clear that Maris and Mantle would chase Ruth in tandem (opposite page). Not clear was whether Mantle (right) or Maris would be able to stand the heat.

connected for his 23rd home run in the Angels opener—Ford's 13th win—and his 24th in the finale off former teammate Ryne Duren.

But with Mantle and Detroit's Norm Cash positioned only three back in the home run derby, most of the attention continued to fall on Maris.

"For a fellow with 27 home runs, Maris was not much in the batting department," wrote Til Ferdenzi of the New York Journal-American in a story reprinted by *The Sporting News*. "He was hitting just .255. Of his first 66 hits, 27 had been homers."

And Ferdenzi couldn't resist prodding Maris for his "ineffectiveness against lefthanded pitchers. Maris had 23 homers against righthanded pitchers and only four against lefties. His overall batting average this year against lefthanders is evidence enough that he would prefer to swing against righthanders every day. He had 11 hits in 67 at-bats ... that's .164."

Maris remained diplomatic as the Yankees finished their 16-game trip with a 44-27 record, good for second place, 1½ games behind Detroit. With the friendly right field porch of Yankee Stadium looming in his immediate future, perceptions could change quickly.

"Well, the figures don't lie," he responded to Ferdenzi. "If you say I've been that lousy against lefties, you must be right."

Yankees Record: 44-27 2nd -1½

WEEK 12		HOME RUN	ON BASE	INN.	OPPONENT (H) OR (A)	PITCHER (THROWS)	GAME	PACE	RUTH'S PACE
JUNE 29					OFF DAY				
JUNE 30	MANTLE	25	1	6	WASHINGTON (H)	DONOVAN (RH)	73	56	55
JULY 1	MANTLE	26	0	2	WASHINGTON (H)	MATHIAS (LH)	74	57	54
	MANTLE	27	2	3	WASHINGTON (H)	MATHIAS (LH)	74	59	54
	MARIS	28	1	9	WASHINGTON (H)	SISLER (RH)	74	62	54
JULY 2	MARIS	29	2	3	WASHINGTON (H)	BURNSIDE (LH)	75	63	54
	MARIS	30	1	7	WASHINGTON (H)	KLIPPSTEIN (RH)	75	65	54
	MANTLE	28	1	8	WASHINGTON (H)	KLIPPSTEIN (RH)	75	61	54
JULY 3					OFF DAY				
JULY 4		–	–	–	DETROIT (H)		76		
	MARIS	31	1	8	DETROIT (H)	LARY (RH)	77	66	52
JULY 5	MARIS	32	0	7	CLEVELAND (H)	FUNK (RH)	78	67	54

Fourth of July week opens with a Mantle bang, closes with a Maris flurry

WEEK

12

June 29 - July 5

It was a simple matter of quality versus quantity. Mickey Mantle liked to wring every last ooh and aah out of a crowd with explosive home runs that traveled well beyond the boundaries of anyone's wildest imagination. Roger Maris was master of the workmanlike homer, those line drives that settled consistently into the 10th row of the right field stands.

This difference in styles was becoming increasingly apparent as Fourth of July week in the Great Home Run Chase unfolded with a Mantle bang and closed with another Maris flurry.

In the opener of a three-game series against Washington at Yankee Stadium, Mantle teed off on a Dick Donovan pitch with Maris on base and hit a towering drive toward the distant center field wall. As Willie Tasby raced back, the ball sailed majestically over his head, banged off the wall just to the right of the 461-foot sign and rebounded over Tasby and back toward the infield. Mantle circled the bases before any Senators player even touched the ball.

Mantle's inside-the-park home run, his 25th, helped Whitey Ford to his American League-leading 14th win. The next day, he added two more

Yankee All-Star selections (left to
right) Whitey Ford, Tony Kubek,
Roger Maris and Mickey Mantle
clown for the cameras before a
July 2 game against Washington.

home runs off lefthander Carl Mathias, the first of which settled into
the left field bleachers, just to the left of the 457-foot sign. With that
blow, Mantle joined Joe DiMaggio and Moose Skowron as the only
players to reach that area twice.

Mantle's second home run of that game was his 27th and tied Maris for
the A.L. lead. But Maris responded with the game's biggest blow, a two-
run, ninth-inning drive into the right field seats that gave the Yankees a
dramatic 7-6 victory.

That home run ended an eight-day drought for Maris, who vaulted back
into the lead with two more homers the next day against Washington,
another in the second game of a July 4 doubleheader against Detroit and

Home runs were flying in a July 2 game against Washington, prompting this postgame celebration by (left to right) Moose Skowron, Maris, Bud Daley, Elston Howard and Mantle. Skowron, Howard and Mantle homered once to support Daley's win while Maris hit two, including No. 29 (above left). Later in the week, Maris (left, left photo) hit No. 32 to support Rollie Sheldon's four-hit pitching in a 6-0 shutout of Cleveland.

his 32nd in the opener of a two-game series against Cleveland. With five homers in as many games, Maris finished the week with a 32-28 lead over his off-field roommate.

Overshadowed by the fusillade was the announcement that Maris, Mantle and shortstop Tony Kubek had been selected to start for the A.L. in the All-Star Game and the intense holiday doubleheader between the first-place Tigers and second-place Yankees. Playing before a crowd of 74,246 at Yankee Stadium, Ford raised his record to 15-2 with a 6-2 victory in the opener, but Detroit bounced back for a 4-3 nightcap win as Yankee killer Frank Lary raised his mark to 12-4.

Yankees Record: 49-28 2nd -½

WEEK 13	HOME RUN	ON BASE	INN.	OPPONENT (H) OR (A)	PITCHER (THROWS)	GAME	PACE	RUTH'S PACE
JULY 6	–	–	–	CLEVELAND (H)		79		
JULY 7	–	–	–	BOSTON (H)		80		
JULY 8 MANTLE	29	0	5	BOSTON (H)	STALLARD (RH)	81	58	55
JULY 9 MARIS	33	0	7	BOSTON (H)	MONBOUQUETTE (RH)	82	66	55
	–	–	–	BOSTON (H)		83		
JULY 10				OFF DAY				
JULY 11				ALL-STAR GAME				
JULY 12				OFF DAY				

◆
WEEK

13

July 6-12

Roger Maris (left) and Mickey Mantle (right) enjoy a quiet moment while awaiting their turn in the batting cage before a July 9 doubleheader against Boston at Yankee Stadium.

Home run race provides fitting backdrop for All-Star Game

It was the All-Star break, the annual rite of summer when baseball pauses to take stock. For major league officials, it was an opportunity to assess the suddenly hot topic of home runs, the issue looming larger with every Roger Maris or Mickey Mantle swing.

"Commissioner Ford Frick soon will call a conference with the Records Committee of the Baseball Writers' Association of America," Dan Daniel reported in the July 13 issue of *The Sporting News*. "The commissioner is quite aroused over the chance that the American League schedule of 162 games, eight more than in past years, will produce records. ... Ford is especially apprehensive about Babe Ruth's record of 60 homers.

"Suppose Roger Maris hits 61 with the help of those extra contests. Suppose, after 154 games, the Yankee right fielder shows only 58 or 59? Yes, even 60? And then totals 61 over the whole season? Frick believes that it would not be right to recognize a mark set after 154 games. The commissioner has strong backing in this attitude."

Maris entered the first of two All-Star breaks with 33 home runs, four more than teammate Mantle and four more than Ruth had hit after 82 games of his record-setting 1927 season. Eyes were focused squarely on the Yankees' right fielder and talk centered around such issues as

EIGHT-MAN SCRAMBLE FOR MVP PRIZES

★ ★ ★ ★ *Specials* .·. *in Most Valuable Derby*

MICKEY MANTLE   NORM CASH   ROGER MARIS   WHITEY FORD

ORLANDO CEPEDA   JOEY JAY   SANDY KOUFAX   FRANK ROBINSON

Pinch-Hitters Pack Payoff Punch

ON THE INSIDE

From Gleamer Page 3

Experts Tab Cash Hottest A. L. Choice

Three Yanks Close Behind; Twirlers Jay and Koufax Among N. L.'s Candidates

By BOB BURNES

ST. LOUIS, Mo.

There's a wide-open race for most valuable honors in both the American and National leagues at the halfway point in the '61 season, a spot check by THE SPORTING NEWS has revealed.

Not only that, but it's a race almost evenly divided between former winners and new contenders and between power hitters and potent pitchers. Four in each league lead the pack.

Two former MVPs — Roger Maris and Mickey Mantle of the Yankees are in the race, but they are competing for honors with some who have never before been accorded this honor. One of these is the slugging Giant, Orlando Cepeda.

Pitcher Whitey Ford of the Yankees, the top hurler in the American League on almost every count except complete games, also is well rated in the competition as the leagues grind to the slowdown point for the first All-Star break.

A step ahead of the three Yankee greats at this moment, however, according to the unofficial poll conducted by THE SPORTING NEWS, is Norm Cash, who is having an astounding season with the Tigers, after failing previously with the White Sox and Indians.

Robinson Sparks Reds' Rise

On the National League side, Cepeda is being offered stiff competition by Frank Robinson, whose bat carried the Reds to the top of the pack, and two young pitchers who have been the sensations of the league in the first half of 1961—Joey Jay of the Reds and Sandy Koufax of the Dodgers.

These eight are by no means the only ones in the thick of the fight for MVP honors.

Considerable backing was found for young John Romano of Cleveland, All-Star catcher and one of the league's top hitters. There were votes also for Harmon Killebrew of Minnesota and Jim Gentile of Baltimore.

These seven were conceded to be far ahead of the rest of the field in the American.

The unofficial first half of the season ended with *The Sporting News* asking its annual question: What players are leading candidates for league MVP awards? Yankees Maris, Mantle and Whitey Ford all got high billing.

expansion, watered-down pitching, longer schedules, lighter bats and, of course, a livelier ball. But still the home runs kept coming.

Mantle's 29th came in a four-homer Yankee blitz that buried Boston 8-5 on July 8, helping Whitey Ford, with relief help from Luis Arroyo, run his record to 16-2. Maris delivered his 33rd the next day in the first game of a Yankee Stadium doubleheader that drew a Sunday afternoon crowd of 47,875. Maris' solo shot helped Rollie Sheldon post a 3-0 victory, but the Red Sox fought back for a 9-6 win in the nightcap. The loss dropped the 53-29 Yankees into second place, a half game behind first-place Detroit, at the break.

Four Yankees flew to San Francisco after the double-header to participate in the first of two 1961 All-Star Games. Maris, Mantle and shortstop Tony Kubek were in the starting lineup at windy Candlestick Park and Maris got the only Yankee hit, a single. Ford was the American League's starting pitcher and worked three innings, giving up one run. The outcome wasn't decided until the 10th inning when, after a series of windblown mishaps, the National League scored twice for a 5-4 win.

"If I had to play 77 games a year in this park, I'd ask to be traded," said an unamused Maris.

Yankees Record: 53-29 2nd -1/2

Center fielder Mantle (7) and right fielder Maris (9) miss connections on a second-inning triple by Pittsburgh's Roberto Clemente (top photos) during the All-Star Game at Candlestick Park. Whitey Ford (left, bottom photo) poses with his 1961 savior, lefty reliever Luis Arroyo.

WEEK 14		HOME RUN	ON BASE	INN.	OPPONENT (H) OR (A)	PITCHER (THROWS)	GAME	PACE	RUTH'S PACE
JULY 13	MARIS	34	1	1	CHICAGO (A)	WYNN (RH)	84	66	55
	MANTLE	30	0	1	CHICAGO (A)	WYNN (RH)	84	58	55
JULY 14	MANTLE	31	0	8	CHICAGO (A)	PIZARRO (LH)	85	59	55
JULY 15	MARIS	35	0	3	CHICAGO (A)	HERBERT (RH)	86	66	54
JULY 16	MANTLE	32	0	4	BALTIMORE (A)	BARBER (LH)	87	60	53
JULY 17	MANTLE	33	0	6	BALTIMORE (A)	PAPPAS (RH)	88	61	53
JULY 18	MANTLE	34	1	1	WASHINGTON (A)	McCLAIN (RH)	89	62	52
	MANTLE	35	0	8	WASHINGTON (A)	McCLAIN (RH)	89	64	52
JULY 19		–	–	–	WASHINGTON (A)		90		
	MANTLE	36	0	6	WASHINGTON (A)	DONOVAN (RH)	91	64	51

Frick rules: Home run record must be set in 154 games

◆

WEEK

14

July 13-19

The 1961 season took an unexpected twist when commissioner Ford Frick (right) jumped into the fray and made life a lot more difficult for Yankee sluggers Roger Maris and Mickey Mantle.

It has been called the "asterisk ruling," but in truth baseball commissioner Ford Frick never used the word on July 17 when he made a controversial announcement that would come to define the 1961 season. What he did say, however, came as an emotional slap to Roger Maris and created a backlash that would torment the Yankees star for the remainder of the season.

"Any player who may hit more than 60 home runs during his club's first 154 games would be recognized as having established a new record," Frick ruled. "However, if the player does not hit more than 60 until after his club has played 154 games, there would have to be some distinctive mark in the record books to show that Babe Ruth's record was set under a 154-game schedule and the total of more than 60 was compiled while a 162-game schedule was in effect. ..."

Frick's ruling was designed to throw a protective screen around Ruth's single-season home run record. The commissioner, a longtime friend and former ghostwriter for Ruth, said he decided to make it formal because of the unusual interest being generated by the home run-hitting exploits of Yankee teammates Maris and Mickey Mantle. But many suspected the decision was more a product of Frick's dismay that

Players sound off on Frick's ruling

Mick 'Wouldn't Want Mark If It Was Set in 155 Games'

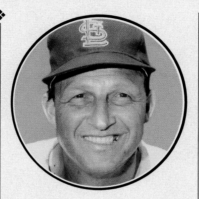

Stan Musial
Cardinals outfielder

"It's a good rule. Baseball records were based on 154-game schedules. Now that we are going to play 162 games in both leagues next season, I think this will lead to having two sets of records. One record for a 154-game season and another for 162 games. ..."

Norm Cash
Tigers first baseman

"If a player is to break Ruth's record, he should do it in the same number of games that Ruth did."

Ernie Banks
Cubs shortstop

"I don't like the ruling. I think the owners make out a schedule for the season. Everything a player does in the season's schedule should be counted in his records."

Roy Sievers
White Sox first baseman

"Why shouldn't it count if one of the players breaks it in a 162-game schedule? The players didn't make the schedule. But there are a couple of players who could break it this year and I'd like to see it done, without restrictions."

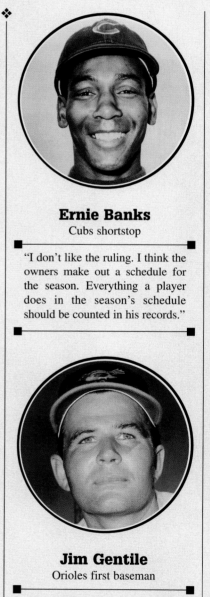

Musial, Cash, Gentile and Spahn Agree Commissioner Made Proper Decision

By HY HURWITZ

BOSTON, Mass.

If the majority rules, then Commissioner Ford Frick made the proper decision when he declared that Babe Ruth's record of 60 homers would not be considered broken unless it's done in 154 games, the schedule played in the American League in 1927 when Ruth set the mark.

During the All-Star Game in Fenway Park, THE SPORTING NEWS polled 17 players from the two circuits. The vote was 12 to 5 in favor of the Frick decision.

Mickey Mantle of the Yankees and elder statesman Stan Musial of the Cardinals were the headliners who favored the Frick verdict. Mantle is generally regarded as having the best chance to fracture the 60 mark, even by his teammate, Roger Maris, who was running one ahead of Mickey when the poll was taken.

"I think it's right," Mantle said, when asked about the commissioner's recent ruling. "Ruth set it in 154 games and you should beat it in the same number of games. If I should break it in the one hundred and fifty-fifth game, I wouldn't want the record."

* * * *

Jim Gentile
Orioles first baseman

"If it's going to be done, it should be done in 154 games. Only two guys have a chance and I think they both could do it in 154 games. I hope so. ..."

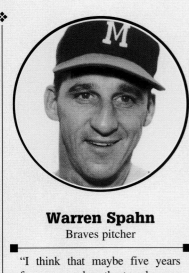

Warren Spahn
Braves pitcher

"I think that maybe five years from now, when the two leagues have expanded to 10 teams and the talent has leveled off, there will be a better chance to break Ruth's record. But in order for it to count, they should do it in 154 games."

Al Kaline
Tigers outfielder

"Whoever hits 61 home runs is entitled to the record, no matter how many games it takes. The owners and leagues made out the schedules and told us how many games we would have to play. So if a record is broken in the official number of games scheduled, it should be a record."

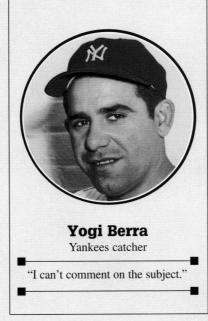

Eddie Mathews
Braves third baseman

"They should make it for 151 games just like the number of games Babe played in when he set the record in 1927. But the regulations should have been put in before the season started and not when a couple of guys get within reach of it."

Whitey Ford
Yankees pitcher

"I'm all for the commissioner's decision. Naturally, I'd like to see a Yankee player break Ruth's record and I think the Babe would, too, if he were still living. But it's got to be done within 154 games or it won't mean anything."

Yogi Berra
Yankees catcher

"I can't comment on the subject."

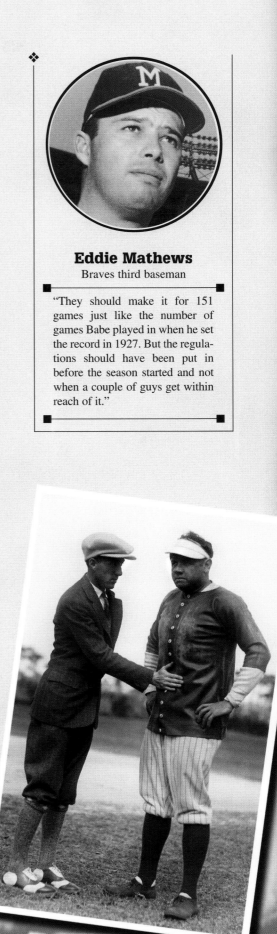

Not lost on critics of the commissioner's ruling was his former association with Babe Ruth, both as a friend and ghostwriter. Frick, dressed in knickers, enjoys a light moment with the Bambino in the mid-1920s.

Maris and Mantle connected back-to-back in the opening inning of a July 13 game at Chicago—No. 34 for Maris and No. 30 for Mantle. Maris gets a warm welcome (above) from Mantle and Mantle is greeted by glad hands in the dugout (right) after his 350th career blast.

Maris (right) discusses hitting technique with a group of interested kids prior to a July 18 game at Washington. Teammate Yogi Berra is an attentive bystander.

Maris, a relative newcomer to the home run-hitting fraternity, would dare to challenge the legendary Bambino.

"I think Mick has a good chance to break it," Maris responded to the ruling. "I think the commissioner shouldn't have made any 154-game ruling when he did. But if Mick breaks it, I hope he does it in 154. The same goes for me."

While Maris' diplomacy was admirable, teammates and friends later confirmed that he simmered over Frick's apparent slight. Mantle also took the diplomatic road, although he, too, was not happy.

"I think it's right," Mantle said of the ruling. "Ruth set it in 154 games and you should beat it in the same number of games. If I should break it in the 155th game, I wouldn't want the record."

Frick received strong support from 37 of 55 baseball writers who responded to a poll by *The Sporting News*. Those who objected did so articulately with several disapproving in part. Most supporters, like

The Lost Homers

July 17 was a momentous day in the 1961 baseball season. Commissioner Ford Frick issued his so-called "asterisk ruling" and Hall of Famer Ty Cobb died, casting a pall over the sport. Lost in that extensive shadow was the second game of a Yankee-Orioles doubleheader at Baltimore that literally changed the course of the Great Home Run Race.

After Mickey Mantle's 33rd home run helped Whitey Ford lift his record to 17-2 in a 5-0 opening win, the Yankees jumped to a 4-1 lead in the nightcap on homers by Mantle, Maris and Clete Boyer. But in the top of the fifth, with the Yankees batting, a drenching rain and lightning streaks filled the sky over Memorial Stadium and sent 44,332 fans running for cover.

The game was eventually called off and the Yankees lost a victory that would have put them in a virtual tie with Detroit for first place. But Maris and Mantle also lost home runs that might well prove significant down the stretch. Maris' 36th would have put him 21 games ahead of Babe Ruth's 1927 record pace and Mantle's 34th would have given him a nine-game edge.

Mantle (left) gets a handshake from Berra after the first of two home runs in a July 18 game at Washington. Maris did not hit a homer that day, but he did make points (above) with Pennsylvania congressman Carroll D. Kearns (center) and New York Rep. Charles E. Goodell.

Frick, argued against the expanded schedule and some even expressed belief that the ruling didn't go far enough.

The ruling came, ironically, in the midst of a seven-home run Mantle week that would give him a 36-35 lead over Maris, who went deep twice. It also came on the day that the death of baseball immortal Ty Cobb snatched newspaper headlines throughout the country.

On the day of the ruling, Mantle hit No. 33 in the opener of a scheduled doubleheader at Baltimore and he tied Maris for the major league lead the next day with two shots in a victory over Washington. Mantle connected for his league-leading 36th on July 19 in the nightcap of a doubleheader against the Senators—his seventh homer in eight games.

With or without Frick's ruling, the dueling sluggers were now front and center on the national baseball stage. Writers and broadcasters were swarming, fans were crowding into parks to see them play and every swing, every off-field move, was being chronicled for posterity. It was exciting, for fans and players alike.

"They are making the most spectacular battle we ever had—I never went through anything nearly so close in my time," said former Yankees great Joe DiMaggio. "I try to catch every game they play, on TV if I can't come up here (to Yankee Stadium)."

Yankees Record: 58-32 T1st —

WEEK 15		HOME RUN	ON BASE	INN.	OPPONENT (H) OR (A)	PITCHER (THROWS)	GAME	PACE	RUTH'S PACE
JULY 20					OFF DAY				
JULY 21	MARIS	36	0	1	BOSTON (A)	MONBOUQUETTE (RH)	92	64	51
	MANTLE	37	0	1	BOSTON (A)	MONBOUQUETTE (RH)	92	66	51
JULY 22		–	–	–	BOSTON (A)		93		
JULY 23		–	–	–	BOSTON (A)		94		
JULY 24					OFF DAY				
JULY 25	MARIS	37	1	4	CHICAGO (H)	BAUMANN (LH)	95	63	54
	MANTLE	38	0	4	CHICAGO (H)	BAUMANN (LH)	95	65	54
	MARIS	38	0	8	CHICAGO (H)	LARSEN (RH)	95	65	54
	MARIS	39	0	4	CHICAGO (H)	KEMMERER (RH)	96	66	53
	MARIS	40	2	6	CHICAGO (H)	HACKER (RH)	96	68	53
JULY 26	MANTLE	39	1	1	CHICAGO (H)	HERBERT (RH)	97	66	53

Maris' doubleheader explosion sends message to skeptical fans

◆
WEEK
15

July 20-26

The *New York Times* called them "seismic tremors," rumbles that rocked Yankee Stadium in fearful succession on the night of July 25. One by one, they shook the Chicago White Sox into submission and lifted 46,240 fans into ranting ecstasy. When Roger Maris hit four home runs and Mickey Mantle one in a 5-1 and 12-0 doubleheader sweep, they served notice that the Great Race would henceforth be run with a new level of drama and intensity.

If this wasn't the turning point of the home run chase, it was at least a message that Maris would not wilt under the mounting pressure. Mantle, to the delight of New York fans who were suddenly embracing him as the legitimate successor to Babe Ruth's Yankee legacy, had taken over the major league lead by hitting eight in a nine-game span, a rampage that left everybody bracing for a Maris fade.

But that didn't happen. Maris connected in the fourth inning of the July 25 opener off lefthander Frank Baumann with Bobby Richardson on base, a drive just inside the right field foul pole. Barely had he settled into the dugout with his 37th home run when Mantle drove a Baumann pitch off the left field foul pole, his 38th.

Roger Maris (right) had reason to smile after reaching the 40 plateau with a four-homer doubleheader against Chicago. When Mickey Mantle homered the next day, their combined total stood at 79 (below).

Maris tied Mantle again with an eighth-inning shot into the right field bleachers off Don Larsen and took over the lead in the nightcap when he connected off Russ Kemmerer and Warren Hacker. Maris finished his big night with five hits, eight RBIs and a long, grueling session with the ever-increasing horde of media representatives. The first-place Yankees finished their night with eight home runs, a 62-33 record and a half-game lead over second-place Detroit.

The eight-home run outburst by New York's M squad (Maris 5, Mantle 3) was one of several interesting stories in Week 15. Whitey Ford raised his record to 18-2 with the help of Maris in the opener of the July 25 doubleheader and the Giants, now located in San Francisco, returned to New York for a July 24 exhibition game. But nobody had a more enjoyable week than reserve catcher Johnny Blanchard.

'Ruth Homer Mark Safe This Season,' Colavito Declares

Sees Day and Night Card as Too Tough

By WATSON SPOELSTRA

DETROIT, Mich.

Rocky Colavito likes the chances of the Tigers to win the American League pennant, but he doesn't think Babe Ruth's swat record of 60 home runs will be broken this year.

As the Tigers completed a tour of the West, Colavito made these observations on the pennant race:

"My guess is that it will take 104 or 105 victories to win it. It's not for me to count out the other clubs. But it looks like it will be us or New York.

"We've got good balance—power, speed and front-line pitching. We've been consistent. We've played at about the same pace all year. I like our chances."

These are the Detroit outfielder's views on the home-run derby: "Several guys in our league are capable of it, but I don't think Ruth's record will be broken. Switching from day ball to night ball and back again is rough. Ruth didn't have to do that."

Who are the American leaguers capable of surpassing Ruth?

Rocky Colavito

Rocky Lists Five Sluggers Who Could Challenge Mark

"Roger Maris and Mickey Mantle, of course," he replied. "Harmon Kill̲ Gentil̲ in a tough park

It was a busy week for Maris and Mantle, who found time to pose (below, left page) with teammate Yogi Berra July 22 and (right) with San Francisco great Willie Mays (center) before a New York exhibition game two days later. Mantle (left) couldn't beat Chicago pitcher Ray Herbert to first base on a July 26 ground ball. But Johnny Blanchard (below) beat every pitcher in sight with a power surge that, temporarily at least, gave him the home run spotlight. Despite eight home runs by Mantle and Maris during a busy week, many skeptics downplayed their chances at a record run.

Pinch hitting in the ninth inning of a July 21 game at Boston, Blanchard hit a two-out grand slam to give the Yankees an 11-8 victory. The next day, Blanchard pinch hit again with two out in the ninth and the Yankees trailing by a run. His homer tied the game and the Yanks went on to score two more for an 11-9 win. On July 26, Blanchard got a start against Chicago and hit two home runs, tying a major league record with four in consecutive at-bats. With Mantle hitting his 39th home run to pull within one of Maris, the Yanks won 5-2.

Blanchard finished his big week with four home runs and seven RBIs—a notch below Maris' 5-and-12 total but ahead of Mantle's 3-and-5. The newest slugging blitz by Maris and Mantle opened a gap in the A.L. home run race with Minnesota's Harmon Killebrew falling to a distant third at 30 and Maris moved ahead of Detroit's Norm Cash in the league RBI race, 96-91. But while the Yankees won five of six games, they couldn't shake the stubborn Tigers in what was shaping up as a two-team sprint to the finish line.

Yankees Record: 63-33 1st +1/2

WEEK 16	HOME RUN	ON BASE	INN.	OPPONENT (H) OR (A)	PITCHER (THROWS)	GAME	PACE	RUTH'S PACE
JULY 27	–	–	–	CHICAGO (H)		98		
JULY 28	–	–	–	BALTIMORE (H)		99		
JULY 29	–	–	–	BALTIMORE (H)		100		
JULY 30	–	–	–	BALTIMORE (H)		101		
	–	–	–	BALTIMORE (H)		102		
JULY 31				ALL-STAR GAME				
AUGUST 1				OFF DAY				
AUGUST 2	–	–	–	KANSAS CITY (H)		103		
MANTLE	40	1	1	KANSAS CITY (H)	DITMAR (RH)	104	63	51

Maris survives injury scare as Mantle pulls even at 40

WEEK

16

July 27 - August 2

The headline in *The Sporting News* sounded an ominous note for the 1961 home run race. "Injury Hoodoo Hits Maris for Third Straight Season," it read, referring to a pulled hamstring that was threatening to send Roger Maris to the Yankees bench.

The scare was legitimate and the hamstring did indeed reduce Maris to a part-time role. Only two days after hitting four home runs in a doubleheader against Chicago, the Yankees right fielder left a game against the White Sox in the third inning after scoring a run. He played the next day against Baltimore, but sat out July 29 and performed pinch-hit duty in the opener of a Sunday doubleheader before returning to the lineup in the nightcap.

"At that point, he had not hit another homer in six Yankee games," TSN reported. "His advantage over Ruth, and fine chance to go into September with 50 or more homers, was fading."

Maris finished Week 16 right where he started—still locked on 40, homerless in eight straight games after a 13-homer July. Mantle was playing, but he, too, was struggling in the long-ball department. His only home run of the week was a monster shot into Yankee Stadium's third deck in right field, a blow that tied Maris at 40 and helped the Yankees complete an August 2 doubleheader sweep of Kansas City.

Mickey Mantle gets an enthusiastic greeting from third base coach Frank Crosetti as he heads home with his 40th home run in a game against Kansas City.

Mantle completed July with 14 home runs.

What the week lacked in home run drama it made up for with interesting developments. The second All-Star Game was played Monday, August 31, at Boston—a 1-1 tie called after nine innings because of rain. This All-Star break was little more than a blip on a schedule that had the Yankees playing a double-header the day before and another two days after. The second twinbill was played without manager Ralph Houk, who was fined $250 and suspended for five days by American League president Joe Cronin for an outburst directed at umpire Ed Hurley during the Sunday doubleheader against Baltimore.

The week's highlight was July 29 when 42,990 fans turned out on a rainy Saturday to enjoy Old-Timers Day festivities and a 5-4 Yankees win over Baltimore.

Yankee Record: 67-36 1st +2½

WEEK 17		HOME RUN	ON BASE	INN.	OPPONENT (H) OR (A)	PITCHER (THROWS)	GAME	PACE	RUTH'S PACE
AUGUST 3		–	–	–	KANSAS CITY (H)		105		
AUGUST 4	MARIS	41	2	1	MINNESOTA (H)	PASCUAL (RH)	106	63	51
AUGUST 5		–	–	–	MINNESOTA (H)		107		
AUGUST 6	MANTLE	41	1	1	MINNESOTA (H)	RAMOS (RH)	108	62	50
	MANTLE	42	0	3	MINNESOTA (H)	RAMOS (RH)	108	63	50
	MANTLE	43	0	2	MINNESOTA (H)	SCHROLL (RH)	109	64	50
AUGUST 7		–	–	–	LOS ANGELES (H)		110		
AUGUST 8		–	–	–	LOS ANGELES (H)		111		
AUGUST 9		–	–	–	LOS ANGELES (H)		112		

Home run fever gets dangerously high as media feeds national frenzy

WEEK

17

August 3-9

With home run fever running dangerously high, Roger Maris and Mickey Mantle entered Week 17 in a 40-40 deadlock. Not only was New York rocking with every Maris and Mantle swing, fans throughout the country were entranced by the notion that Babe Ruth's single-season home run record might finally fall. The media did everything within its power to feed the frenzy.

"You would be amazed at the interest, worldwide, in the Mantle-Maris home run rivalry," former Yankees great Joe DiMaggio told Dan Daniel in the August 16 issue of *The Sporting News*. "It is even greater than the one between Ruth and Lou Gehrig in 1927. That season the Babe set his mark of 60 and Lou got 47.

"Now we find Mickey and Roger neck and neck, sportswriters playing up the possibility of a new record and the commissioner ruling that no new mark will be recognized unless it is done inside 154 games. ... I visit service installations all over the world ... Army officers keep asking me, 'Can Maris do it?' "

On sports pages throughout the country, the Maris-Mantle home run derby was being chronicled and analyzed by daily charts showing such things as game comparisons to Ruth, numbers versus lefthanded and righthanded pitchers and season pace. Scientific tests were being conducted to determine whether the 1961 ball was livelier than its 1927

New York fans had plenty to cheer about August 4 when Roger Maris (above left) hit home run No. 41, Luis Arroyo (center) raised his record to 9-3 with a relief win and Johnny Blanchard hit a game-winning, 10th-inning home run against Minnesota. Maris did have his bad moments, such as a strikeout (right) in an August 9 game against Los Angeles.

counterpart, fan polls and contests were being offered, relative merits of 1961 and 1927 pitchers were being debated and editors, even from such non-sports publications as *Newsweek*, were clamoring for up-close-and-personal looks at the nation's two hottest personalities.

With the expanding interest came questions, questions and more questions, which Mantle and Maris answered over and over in long interview sessions before and after games. Adding to the Mantle-Maris drama was the success of the Yankees, Whitey Ford's 19-2 record, Johnny Blanchard's late-game heroics, Luis Arroyo's emergence as a dominating closer and catcher Elston Howard's surprising run at an American League batting title.

Mantle (right) avoids the tag of Angels catcher Del Rice to score a first-inning run in an August 8 game at Yankee Stadium. The interested spectator (above) is Merlyn Mantle, who was in town to encourage her husband in his record pursuit. Mantle and Maris (below) check the lineup card with manager Ralph Houk (center) before the August 9 game.

When asked what he told questioners who asked whether Maris could top the Babe, DiMaggio said he told them "they were forgetting the man with the better chance. Obviously, Mantle, a switch hitter, has a big edge over Maris, who admits he has a weakness against lefthanders."

Almost on cue, Mantle bolted into the lead August 6 with a three-home run doubleheader before 39,408 fans at Yankee Stadium. After Maris had taken the lead with his 41st two days earlier against Minnesota, Mantle connected in the first and third innings of the opener—a 7-6 win in 15 innings—off Twins righthander Pedro Ramos to move back ahead. He added a solo shot off Al Schroll (No. 43) in the nightcap, a 3-2 Yankees win.

While the sluggers managed only four home runs, the week was significant in other ways. Ford, stuck on 19 wins, missed

in his second attempt to get No. 20 in the 15-inning win over Minnesota. The Yankees extended their win streak to seven by week's end and widened their A.L. lead over Detroit to three games. Arroyo lifted his record to 10-3 with relief wins over Minnesota and Los Angeles, Blanchard won another game with a three-run 10th-inning homer, Maris and Mantle reached the 100-RBI plateau and Howard lifted his average to .362, second only to Detroit's Norm Cash.

Yankees Record: 74-37   1st   +3

Another Research Reveals Ruth Mark as Real McCoy

By HAL LEBOVITZ
CLEVELAND, O.

After careful research, it has been substantiated that Babe Ruth did not hit any "phony" home runs when he socked his record 60.

He did NOT bounce any where else, though a ball bo

He did NOT benefit fro right field pavilion in St.

week's issue of THE SPORT went far above and beyond

So Ruth did not take record. Rather, instead of some because of the diff

Foxx Was Speediest in Flogging 41 HRs

Jim Reached Milestone in Ninety-Ninth Game in '32; Babe Needed 124 Tilts in '27, Greenberg 110 in '38

By JOE KING
NEW YORK, N. Y.

Both Mickey Mantle and Roger Maris entered the home stretch of the final 20 homers en route to Babe Ruth's record of 60 in early August, much before the Babe himself hit No. 41.

However, Jimmie Foxx was the early bird of them all when he hit 58 in 1932. Double-X had No. 41 in his ninety-ninth game. Hank Greenberg, who also hit 5 in 1938, had No. 41 in 110 games. The N. L. lead

WEEK 18		HOME RUN	ON BASE	INN.	OPPONENT (H) OR (A)	PITCHER (THROWS)	GAME	PACE	RUTH'S PACE
AUGUST 10		–	–	–	LOS ANGELES (H)		113		
AUGUST 11	MARIS	42	0	5	WASHINGTON (A)	BURNSIDE (LH)	114	60	50
	MANTLE	44	1	7	WASHINGTON (A)	BURNSIDE (LH)	114	63	50
AUGUST 12	MARIS	43	0	4	WASHINGTON (A)	DONOVAN (RH)	115	61	51
AUGUST 13	MARIS	44	0	4	WASHINGTON (A)	DANIELS (RH)	116	62	51
	MANTLE	45	0	9	WASHINGTON (A)	DANIELS (RH)	116	63	51
	MARIS	45	1	1	WASHINGTON (A)	KUTYNA (RH)	117	63	50
AUGUST 14					OFF DAY				
AUGUST 15	MARIS	46	0	4	CHICAGO (H)	PIZARRO (LH)	118	64	51
AUGUST 16	MARIS	47	1	1	CHICAGO (H)	PIERCE (LH)	119	64	51
	MARIS	48	1	3	CHICAGO (H)	PIERCE (LH)	119	66	51

Maris explodes, moves to top of home run leaderboard

◆
WEEK

18

August 10-16

Roger Maris (right) watches the flight of his 47th home run in an August 16 game against Chicago. Maris also hit No. 48 in the game at Yankee Stadium.

It was the calm before the storm. When Whitey Ford earned a 3-1 victory over Los Angeles August 10, becoming a 20-game winner for the first time and extending the Yankees' winning streak to eight games, Roger Maris was lurking quietly in the background, a fading challenger to Babe Ruth's single-season home run record. Six days later, the talented right fielder would be at the center of the baseball universe.

Ford's victory was significant for several reasons. It was his 14th in a row, it lifted his record to an incredible 20-2 and it was only the fourth without the aid of a Maris or Mickey Mantle home run. Maris had homered eight times in Ford wins, Mantle 10. But that duo had managed only four hits in 26 at-bats in their four-game series against the Angels and Maris had hit only one home run in his last 17 games, falling two behind Mantle in the home run race.

That drought ended the next day against Washington lefthander Pete Burnside when Maris connected for No. 42. He then hit a home run in each of the next three games against the Senators and three more in the first two games of a series against Chicago—seven in a six-game stretch and his 11th, 12th and 13th of the season against White Sox pitching.

"His numbers 46, 47 and 48 wallops were doubly significant because they came off southpaw hurling (one off Juan Pizarro, two off Billy

Pierce), a diet which supposedly does not agree with Roger," Dan Daniel wrote in *The Sporting News*. "Ten of his 48 were at the expense of lefties."

The blitz put Maris 15 games ahead of Ruth's pace in 1927, a season in which the Bambino connected 17 times in September. Mantle homered twice against Washington to raise his total to 45, 13 games ahead of Ruth after 119 games. The Maris-Mantle combination of 93 tied them for second place on the all-time list of teammate home runs—14 behind Ruth and Lou Gehrig, who combined for 107 in 1927.

Not only did Maris break out of his home run funk, he did it with a Mantle-like flair. His August 11 homer against Washington was a towering shot over the right-center field fence that hit a Griffith Stadium light tower and bounded back onto the field. His home run in the first game of an August 13 doubleheader traveled 450 feet, rammed against the outer wall and landed in the bullpen to the right of center field. It was the farthest a ball could be hit at Griffith and still stay in the park.

Maris' August 15 home run against Chicago at Yankee Stadium was a skyscraper that had to face the problem of re-entry and both of his shots in an August 16 win over the White Sox landed in the upper deck.

But not even a Maris home run and the superb relief work of Luis Arroyo could prevent the inevitable—Ford dropped a 2-1 decision to the White Sox on August 15, ending his 14-game win streak. The first-place Yankees ended a 4-3 week a day later with a 78-40 record, good for a three-game lead over second-place Detroit.

Celebrities were everywhere as hungry photographers looked for new material on the Maris-Mantle home run chase. The two Yankee sluggers took time to pose (top photo) with Claire Ruth, widow of legendary Bambino, and former 50-homer slugger Ralph Kiner (above).

Yankees Record: 78-40 1st +3

Blase Broadway Buzzing Over Maris, Mantle HRs

In a busy home run week, Maris and Mantle found themselves deadlocked briefly at 44 home runs (top photo) and then at 45, which they took time to acknowledge (right) after an August 13 doubleheader split with Washington. The stirring battle generated attention-grabbing headlines throughout the country.

WEEK 19		HOME RUN	ON BASE	INN.	OPPONENT (H) OR (A)	PITCHER (THROWS)	GAME	PACE	RUTH'S PACE
AUGUST 17		–	–	–	CHICAGO (H)		120		
AUGUST 18		–	–	–	CLEVELAND (A)		121		
AUGUST 19		–	–	–	CLEVELAND (A)		122		
AUGUST 20	MANTLE	46	2	1	CLEVELAND (A)	J. PERRY (RH)	123	61	50
	MARIS	49	1	3	CLEVELAND (A)	J. PERRY (RH)	123	65	50
		–	–	–	CLEVELAND (A)		124		
AUGUST 21					OFF DAY				
AUGUST 22	MARIS	50	1	6	LOS ANGELES (A)	McBRIDE (RH)	125	65	52
AUGUST 23		–	–	–	LOS ANGELES (A)		126		

Maris delivers his 50th home run in a Hollywood-worthy script

WEEK

19

August 17-23

While Week 19 did not rank among Roger Maris' most prolific in the home run column, it was momentous in several other ways. The two homers he did hit put him in select company and news he received from his Kansas City-area home rejuvenated his mentally tired body.

Playing in Cleveland while wife Pat was on the verge of delivering their fourth child, Maris hit his 49th home run to the delight of 56,307 Cleveland fans in the opener of a Sunday doubleheader. Mickey Mantle connected for his 46th in the same game and the M&M boys drove in all the Yankee runs in Ralph Terry's 6-0 victory.

After the Yankees had completed their sweep of the Indians with a 5-2 win, they flew Monday to Los Angeles, where Maris received news that he was the father of another boy, his third. Assured that everything was up to date in Kansas City, the Yankees' next stop after Los Angeles, Maris celebrated by hitting his 50th home run in a Tuesday battle against the Angels at Wrigley Field.

"The man has been great all season," marveled Yankees manager Ralph Houk after watching Maris become the eighth player in history to reach the 50 plateau and the first to make it before September 1. But his two-run, sixth-inning drive over the center field fence off righthander Ken

Roger Maris, his eyes fixed on the flight of home run No. 50, leaves the batter's box after connecting off Angels righthander Ken McBride. Also watching the ball is catcher Earl Averill.

McBride couldn't avert a loss that allowed Detroit to pull within two games of the American League lead.

The focus of Week 19 centered squarely on home runs. With the Cincinnati Reds and Los Angeles Dodgers engaged in a tight National League pennant race and the Yankees fighting to hold off the Tigers, Maris and Mantle dominated almost every baseball conversation throughout the country.

"Naturally, we are reminded of the home run race the moment we come on the field for pre-game practice and are pelted with questions by columnists, magazine writers and radio commentators," Houk said.

Yanks Hitch Belts for Hot Fight All the Way to Wire

'Walks Will Stymie Maris,' Kiner Predicts

Bambino Had His Share of Patsy Chuckers in '27

Mantle, homerless in five straight games, tosses his bat (above) after flying out to end a 5-1 Yankee loss at Cleveland. As Maris' home run total reached 50, headlines showed how focused the baseball world was on New York.

"But in that clubhouse, by ourselves, I can assure you everyone, and that goes double for Maris and Mantle, is thinking of only one thing—the winning of the pennant."

For Maris and Mantle, the magnitude of the chase was shocking. Everywhere they went they were besieged by admiring fans, every moment in the clubhouse was devoted to quenching the appetite of a hungry media and every move on the field was noted and recorded. Batting practice had become an event. Record crowds were turning out

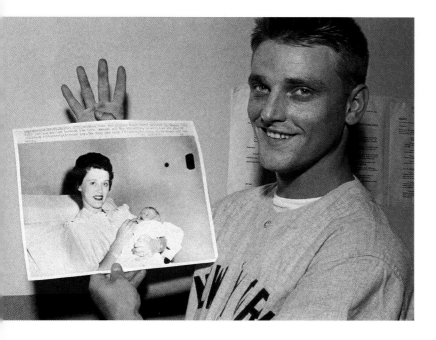

for every game, home and away. The chasers were becoming the chasees.

And everybody had theories and opinions.

"The pitchers are going to stop Maris," predicted former slugger Ralph Kiner, a member of the 50-homer club. "And I'll tell you how. They'll start walking him."

"The bats are lighter, more easily maneuvered," offered A.L. president Joe Cronin. "The old notion that you need a bat weighing from 40 to 50 ounces to produce homers has been destroyed."

Maris had reason to celebrate August 22 after learning he was a father for the fourth time. Maris (above) holds up a wire service picture of his wife Pat with their new son and poses (right) with a bat engraved with the good news. Maris was with the Yankees in Los Angeles while his family was home in Kansas City.

For those who pointed to the weak pitching of an expanded American League, *The Sporting News* pointed out that Ruth in 1927 feasted on pitchers from a Boston team that won 10 fewer games and lost more than either 1961 expansion team.

The *New York Times* went so far as to ask Casey, an IBM 1401 computer based at the Statistical Tabulating Corporation, whether either

Mantle and Maris both hit home runs in the first game of a doubleheader in Cleveland, helping Ralph Terry raise his record to 10-1. Mantle (top left, opposite page) was greeted by Maris after his 46th homer in the first inning and Maris (top right, opposite page) was greeted by Mantle after his 49th in the third. Both players celebrated with Terry (above center) after the game. Mantle also showed off his glove work (left) when he raced in to make a shoestring catch in an August 17 game against Chicago at Yankee Stadium.

player could break Ruth's record. The answer was Maris yes, Mantle no—a prediction that merited a four-column head.

Lost in the Mantle-Maris glare was a Yankee winning spree that lifted the team to 41 games over .500. From June 4 through August 23, the Yankees had played at a .720 clip, winning 59 of 82 games. Whitey Ford was 21-3, Luis Arroyo 11-3, Ralph Terry 10-1, Rollie Sheldon 9-3 and Jim Coates 9-4. Catcher Elston Howard (.354) and Mantle (.320) ranked second and fifth on the A.L. batting charts, Maris (117) and Mantle (112) ranked 1-2 in RBIs and the Bronx Bombers were well on their way to a team record for home runs.

If all wasn't right in New York, it was awfully close.

Yankees Record: 83-42   1st   +3

WEEK 20	HOME RUN	ON BASE	INN.	OPPONENT (H) OR (A)	PITCHER (THROWS)	GAME	PACE	RUTH'S PACE
AUGUST 24	–	–	–	LOS ANGELES (A)		127		
AUGUST 25	–	–	–	KANSAS CITY (A)		128		
AUGUST 26 MARIS	51	0	6	KANSAS CITY (A)	WALKER (RH)	129	64	53
AUGUST 27	–	–	–	KANSAS CITY (A)		130		
AUGUST 28				OFF DAY				
AUGUST 29	–	–	–	MINNESOTA (A)		131		
AUGUST 30 MANTLE	47	0	7	MINNESOTA (A)	KAAT (LH)	132	58	54

Countdown to 154 is on as Maris struggles to cope with celebrity

WEEK

20

August 24-30

As the last leg of his home run odyssey began with a whimper, Roger Maris talked and acted like a beaten man. "I'm tired. I'll be glad when the season is over," he told the relentless barrage of reporters who peppered him with questions before every game and then huddled around him for hours after like hungry vultures.

"Roger answers a thousand questions a day from newspapermen, broadcasters, magazine writers and others," said concerned Yankees manager Ralph Houk. "Generally the questions run to a pattern but there are a few smart alecks who have put words in his mouth and who give a misleading twist to what he says. That certainly bothers him."

When a Kansas City newspaper printed Maris' local Raytown address while the Yankees were in town, the result was predictable. "When we got up that morning," Maris said, "our street looked like the Los Angeles freeway."

The frenzy also manifested itself in positive ways. In the Yankees' final game at Los Angeles' Wrigley Field, a capacity crowd of 19,819 turned out to see Maris and Mickey Mantle. Their next game attracted a Kansas City season-record crowd of 30,830, their second game against the A's brought in 32,149 and the third a Municipal Stadium-record 34,065. Consecutive games in Minneapolis set Metropolitan Stadium records with crowds of 40,118 and 41,357.

Mickey Mantle (above) connects with a pitch from Minnesota's Jim Kaat for home run No. 47—his first in nine games. Waiting for the errant pitch is catcher Earl Battey. Mantle's home run helped Yankees pitcher Bill Stafford (right) record his 12th victory, a 4-0 shutout.

Under such pressure, Maris hit his 51st home run in an August 26 game against the Athletics—a solo blast over the right-center field fence that put him within nine of Babe Ruth's single-season record. With 26 games remaining in commissioner Ford Frick's 154-game decree, the countdown was on.

The clock also was ticking on Mantle, who fell five behind his teammate before breaking a frustrating home run drought with a solo blast on August 30 against the Twins. Before driving a Jim Kaat pitch into the left field bleachers, Mantle had connected only once in 15 games. The 154 rule and other controversies weighed heavy on his mind.

"I say if Roger Maris breaks Babe Ruth's record of 60 homers, he should receive full credit," Mantle said in a *New York Times* interview. "It is unfair to belittle his effort with such criticism as the ball is livelier, the bats are lighter and so on.

"All I know is I'm hitting the ball as hard as ever this year but I'm not getting the distance I did four or five years ago and I'm not hitting as well for average. Why? Because the pitchers are slicker and smarter

The trip to Los Angeles afforded sluggers-turned-movie stars (right photo, left to right) Yogi Berra, Mantle and Maris the chance to meet actress Doris Day, with whom they were to appear in a motion picture called "A Touch of Mink." In Minneapolis, Maris struggled to get back his home run stroke against such pitchers as Camilo Pascual (opposite page) and Jim Kaat.

Mantle, Maris and Berra Get Roles in Hollywood Comedy

HOLLYWOOD, Calif.—No one is rooting harder for Mickey Mantle and Roger Maris to break Babe Ruth's home-run record than officials of Revue Studio here. Should either of the Yankee sluggers, or both, achieve the feat, executives of the studio predict a smash success for a film now in production.

Mantle and Maris, along with Yogi Berra, will have roles in "Touch of Mink," a comedy starring Cary Grant and Doris Day and scheduled for release shortly after the close of the season.

The scene in which the players will appear will be filmed at the studio here in a replica of the Yankee dugout at Yankee Stadium. It will be shot during the Yankees' series with the Angels

than they were before. I know they are a lot better than when I came up 10 years ago."

Despite the distractions, the Yankees won four of six games on the road and braced for a Labor Day series at Yankee Stadium against the Tigers, who were only 2½ games back and hanging tough. Ford lifted his record to 22-3 at Kansas City with the help of home runs by Elston Howard and Yogi Berra and Ralph Terry won twice, lifting his mark to 11-2.

The irony of the week concerned the Maris-Mantle race. In the Yankees' nine games at tiny Wrigley Field, home of the expansion Los Angeles Angels, the sluggers had managed only two home runs apiece— far below what so-called baseball experts had predicted.

Yankees Record: 87-44 1st +2½

WEEK 21		HOME RUN	ON BASE	INN.	OPPONENT (H) OR (A)	PITCHER (THROWS)	GAME	PACE	RUTH'S PACE
AUGUST 31	MANTLE	48	0	4	MINNESOTA (A)	KRALICK (LH)	133	59	55
SEPT. 1		–	–	–	DETROIT (H)		134		
SEPT. 2	MARIS	52	0	6	DETROIT (H)	LARY (RH)	135	63	56
	MARIS	53	1	8	DETROIT (H)	AGUIRRE (LH)	135	64	56
SEPT. 3	MANTLE	49	1	1	DETROIT (H)	BUNNING (RH)	136	59	56
	MANTLE	50	0	9	DETROIT (H)	STALEY (RH)	136	60	56
SEPT. 4		–	–	–	WASHINGTON (H)		137		
		–	–	–	WASHINGTON (H)		138		
SEPT. 5	MANTLE	51	0	2	WASHINGTON (H)	McCLAIN (RH)	139	60	57
SEPT. 6	MARIS	54	0	4	WASHINGTON (H)	CHENEY (RH)	140	63	58

Yankees sweep aside Tigers, return focus to the home run race

WEEK

21

August 31 - September 6

For 72 hours over Labor Day weekend in New York City, the tight American League pennant race threatened to relegate the home run derby to second billing on the baseball marquee. But nothing, it seemed, not even a pulsating three-game series against second-place Detroit, could overcome the growing drama of the Roger Maris and Mickey Mantle show.

For one day, at least, it tried. The series opened with a pitching masterpiece, Whitey Ford matched against Detroit lefthander Don Mossi with the Yankees holding a precarious 1½-game lead. With 65,566 fans packing Yankee Stadium, Ford and Bud Daley shut down the Tigers on seven hits and left fielder Yogi Berra thwarted an eighth-inning Tigers rally with a throw from the left field corner that nailed Al Kaline at second base. Mossi held the Yanks in check until the ninth inning, when first baseman Bill Skowron singled home the game's only run.

Maris and Mantle were 0-for-8 in the opener, but that would change. Maris hit a tie-breaking sixth-inning home run the next day off Yankee killer Frank Lary and added a two-run shot in the eighth off lefthander Hank Aguirre to key a 7-2 victory that lifted Ralph Terry to 12-2. Homers 52 and 53 sent the crowd of 50,261 into a frenzy and gave Maris distinction as the second Yankee (behind only Babe Ruth) to hit that many in a season.

Bat is about to meet ball (above) and the result will be Roger Maris' 54th home run. Washington pitcher Tom Cheney (right) looks discouraged as Maris rounds the bases and helps secure Whitey Ford's 23rd victory in the September 6 game at Yankee Stadium.

Japanese Journal Giving Double-O to M and M Race

By DAN DANIEL
NEW YORK, N. Y.

The Roger Maris-Mickey Mantle home-run excitement is getting quite a play in newspapers in Japan. The trend of thinking over there is indicated by a list of 18 questions compiled by the managing director of the Hochi Shimbun, and offered to Roger Maris by a representative of that paper.

Maris listened to the 18 questions intently and replied, "Mantle will pass me. That seems to answer them all."

Here are the questions from the Nipponese Newsman:

1. How does it feel for you to go after Babe Ruth's record?
2. What method of attack do you think is best to break any home-run hitting slump?
3. What is giving you strength in your home-run race today?
4. Are opposing pitchers deliberately walking you?
5. Is deliberate walking upsetting your co-ordi-

Game 3 belonged to Mantle, who wasn't even expected to play. Battling an arm injury that affected his swing, the Mick delighted 55,676 fans with a two-run homer in the first inning and a game-tying solo shot in the ninth, his 50th of the season. The Yankees won 8-5 a few minutes later when catcher Elston Howard lined a two-out, three-run shot into the left field seats, making a winner of sturdy reliever Luis Arroyo (13-3).

The three wins gave the Yankees firm command of the American League and sent the Tigers reeling. The New Yorkers stretched their winning streak to seven with a four-game sweep of Washington while Detroit dropped three straight to Baltimore. By week's end the Yankees' lead was eight games.

But much of the post-Detroit series spotlight focused on Mantle, who continued to nurse his injured left forearm. "He was hurt. He kept putting ice on his arm during the game," Houk marveled. "But he had a pretty good day for a guy with a bad arm, didn't he?"

Mantle just winked and smiled when asked about the injury. "It shortened my swing," he said. But swelling forced him out of the lineup and

Mantle (above) is greeted by Elston Howard after hitting his 48th home run in at loss at Minnesota and Maris (right) watches the flight of home run 52, the first of two he would hit in a September 2 win over Detroit. Game 1 of the critical Detroit series did not start well when ace Whitey Ford (top right) had to be removed by manager Ralph Houk in the fifth inning, but the Yankees won anyway and launched their pennant-deciding 13-game winning streak.

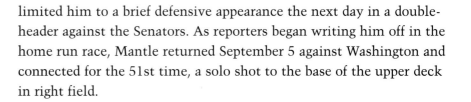
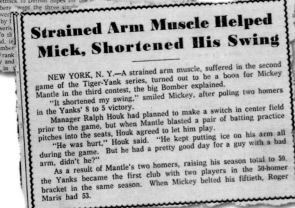
limited him to a brief defensive appearance the next day in a double-header against the Senators. As reporters began writing him off in the home run race, Mantle returned September 5 against Washington and connected for the 51st time, a solo shot to the base of the upper deck in right field.

While lacking Mantle's dramatic flair, Maris continued his march toward Ruth's magic "60" with his 54th home run September 6 against the Senators. Maris connected with the bases empty off righthander Tom Cheney in the fourth inning of an 8-0 victory that also featured two home runs by Johnny Blanchard, one apiece by Bill Skowron and Bob Hale and Whitey Ford's 23rd win in 26 decisions.

Maris' home run, in his 140th game, snapped a 16 at-bat hitless streak and left him six short of Ruth with 15 games remaining in the 154-game limit (155 with the early season tie) prescribed by commissioner Ford Frick. By week's end, Maris and Mantle had combined for 105 home runs, two short of the teammate record of 107 set by Ruth and Lou Gehrig in 1927, and stood as the first teammates to reach the 50 plateau in the same season.

Their total accounted for half of the Yankees' A.L.-record team total of 210.

Yankees Record: 94-45   1st   +8

Maris and Mantle took time
before their September 4 game
at Washington to discuss the home
run race with former President Harry
Truman (above). Then Maris crossed
everybody up by dropping down
a bunt (left) against the Senators.
Yankees (right photo, left to right)
Elston Howard, Mantle and pitcher
Jim Coates had reason to celebrate
after starring in a 6-1 September 5
win at Washington.

WEEK 22		HOME RUN	ON BASE	INN.	OPPONENT (H) OR (A)	PITCHER (THROWS)	GAME	PACE	RUTH'S PACE
SEPT. 7	MARIS	55	0	3	CLEVELAND (H)	STIGMAN (LH)	141	64	57
SEPT. 8	MANTLE	52	0	5	CLEVELAND (H)	BELL (RH)	142	60	57
SEPT. 9	MARIS	56	0	7	CLEVELAND (H)	GRANT (RH)	143	64	57
SEPT. 10		–	–	–	CLEVELAND (H)		144		
	MANTLE	53	0	3	CLEVELAND (H)	J. PERRY (RH)	145	60	57
SEPT. 11					OFF DAY				
SEPT. 12		–	–	–	CHICAGO (A)		146		
SEPT. 13					RAINOUT				

Pressure mounts for Maris as 154-game deadline looms

Home run No. 55 came September 7 against Cleveland and put Roger Maris (right) in a celebratory mood.

"Hey Roger, do you think you'll hit 60?"

"Mick, how about a picture of you and Roger posing with crossed bats?"

"Do you think Frick's 154-game ruling is fair?" "How do you feel about beating the Babe?" "What's your favorite color?"

So began, and ended, a typical work day in the life of Yankee sluggers Roger Maris and Mickey Mantle in the late summer of 1961. Questions they had patiently answered over and over came fast and furious, always delivered enthusiastically by a new face in the crowd. Photo requests that had been filled a hundred times came with a naive sense of originality.

Once Maris and Mantle stepped outside the Queens apartment they shared with reserve outfielder Bob Cerv, everything seemed to be fair game for hungry fans and media.

"You can't have a private life," Mantle told a *New York Times* reporter before a September 9 game against Cleveland at Yankee Stadium. "It's just impossible. Everywhere you go, people think they know you."

"I don't want to talk about it," said Cerv when asked for the umpteenth time about the off-field activities of his famous roommates.

Maris (above, opposite page) had reason to smile after hitting his 56th home run (above) in a September 9 game against the Indians. The chart (opposite page) showed Maris' 143-game progress against Ruth's 1927 final numbers.

"Their private life is nobody's business, right? That's why we moved out there—to get away from all that nonsense."

As the constant barrage of questions began eating away at the sensitive Maris, his answers became tart and monosyllabic, mood swings became more apparent and he lashed out in ways he normally would have abhorred.

"Soar is usually a good umpire," he said in an unusual outburst directed at veteran umpire Hank Soar after a homerless performance in

RUTH		MARIS
32	AGE	27
251	WEIGHT	200
42 oz.	BAT	33 oz.
.356	BATTING AVERAGE	.272
164	RUNS BATTED IN	132
60	HOME RUNS	56

a September 12 game at Chicago. "Soar called some very bad pitches against me."

When asked how he felt about losing one or two at-bats when that game was called because of rain in the sixth inning with the Yankees leading 4-3, he shot back, "Look, right now winning the pennant is as important to me as breaking that record. It'll be all right with me if, from now until the end of the season, we are rained out in the sixth inning of every ball game in which we are leading."

Maris' agitation seemed to grow with every question and the mounting tension manifested itself in other ways. Every missed home run opportunity added to the strain.

"He is so tight up there at the plate that he can hardly breathe," Soar responded when told of Maris' critical comments. "I have no intention of getting into an argument with him, but I certainly am not going to let him put the blame on me. He seems to think that every pitch he doesn't swing at is a ball. ... Maris is really a nice kid, but he's under terrific pressure now."

Former Yankees great Phil Rizzuto, who watched Maris' record crusade from the broadcast booth, agreed. "Here was a kid who was so misunderstood," Rizzuto recalled years later. "Everybody was rooting for Mantle to break the home run record. Poor Maris—he didn't know how to handle the press. They hounded him."

Amid reports that an overwrought Maris was losing hair and had developed a mysterious rash, he continued his march toward destiny. Home run No. 55 came in the third inning of a September 7 victory over Cleveland, a solo shot that helped Ralph Terry raise his record to 13-2. No. 56 came two days later in an 8-7 win over the Indians that featured a four-run ninth-inning rally by the Yankees.

Mantle, battling his usual leg injuries and a late-week bout with the flu, stayed alive by hitting his 52nd (September 8) and 53rd (September 10) home runs, also in wins over Cleveland. When the week ended with a 4-2 victory over Chicago—the Yankees' 13th straight win—both players had nine games remaining in the 154-game deadline (155 because of a tie) that commissioner Ford Frick had set to beat Ruth's single-season record. The still-controversial 154-game edict.

"I do not wish to become involved in a dispute with Ford, but I can see no logic in the ruling that if Ruth's record is to be topped, it must be excelled inside 154 decisions," said American League president Joe Cronin. "I certainly respect the commissioner's feelings about the matter, but so far as I'm concerned it will be a new official record if either or both do it in the 162 games."

Frick answered quickly.

"Sure, it would be a record if done in 162 games. I never said it wouldn't," he said. "I don't know what the misunderstanding's about. I don't care what Mr. Cronin says. There will be two records if it happens in 162. One will say, 'Most homers in a season,

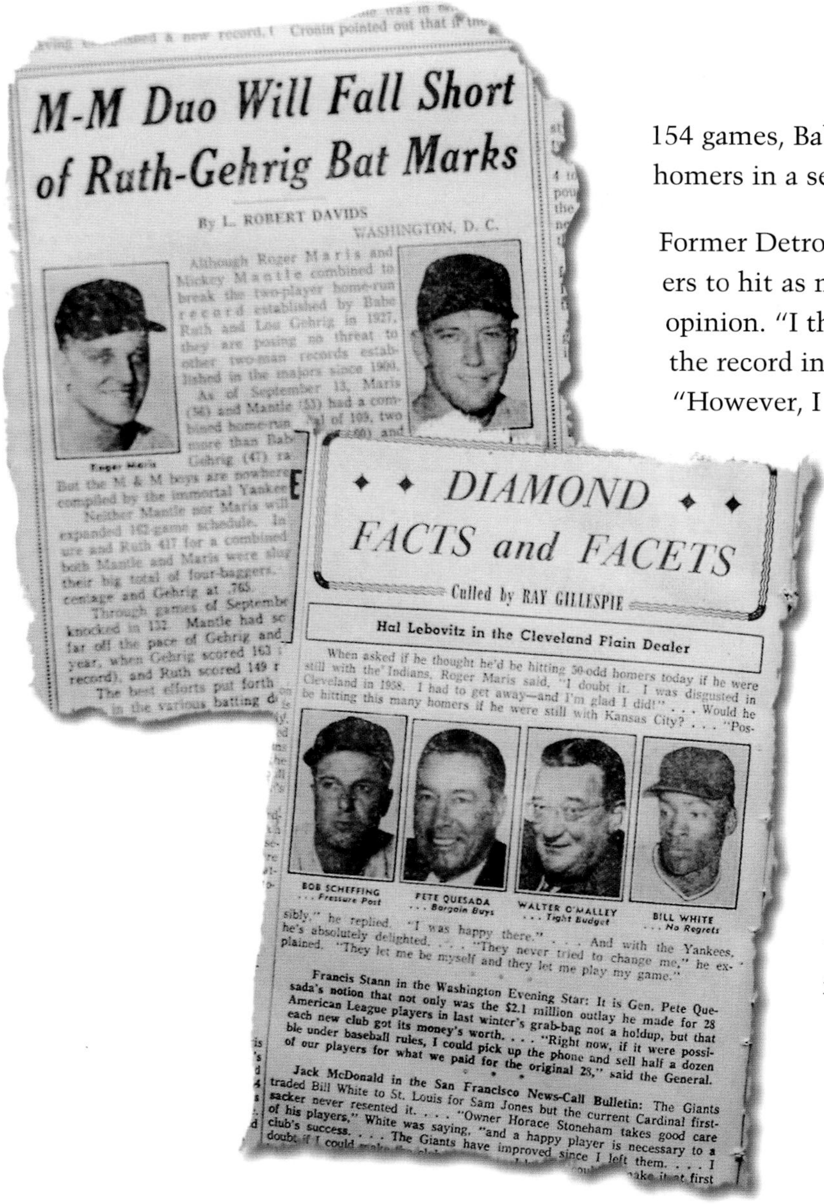

M-M Duo Will Fall Short of Ruth-Gehrig Bat Marks

By L. ROBERT DAVIDS
WASHINGTON, D. C.

Although Roger Maris and Mickey Mantle combined to break the two-player home-run record established by Babe Ruth and Lou Gehrig in 1927, they are posing no threat to other two-man records established in the majors since 1900.

As of September 13, Maris (56) and Mantle (53) had a combined home-run ... of 109, two more than Babe ... (60) and Gehrig (47) ...

Roger Maris

But the M & M boys are nowhere ... compiled by the immortal Yankee...

Neither Mantle nor Maris will ... expanded 162-game schedule. In ... ure and Ruth 417 for a combined ... both Mantle and Maris were slug... their big total of four-baggers. ... centage and Gehrig at .765.

Through games of Septembe... knocked in 132. Mantle had sc... far off the pace of Gehrig and ... year, when Gehrig scored 163 ... record), and Ruth scored 149 r...

The best efforts put forth ... in the various batting d...

◆ ◆ DIAMOND ◆ ◆ FACTS and FACETS

Culled by RAY GILLESPIE

Hal Lebovitz in the Cleveland Plain Dealer

When asked if he thought he'd be hitting 50-odd homers today if he were still with the Indians, Roger Maris said, "I doubt it. I was disgusted in Cleveland in 1958. I had to get away—and I'm glad I did!" . . . Would he be hitting this many homers if he were still with Kansas City? . . . "Possibly," he replied. "I was happy there." . . . And with the Yankees, he's absolutely delighted. . . . "They never tried to change me," he explained. "They let me be myself and they let me play my game."

BOB SCHEFFING . . . Pressure Post
PETE QUESADA . . . Bargain Buys
WALTER O'MALLEY . . . Tight Budget
BILL WHITE . . . No Regrets

* * *

Francis Stann in the Washington Evening Star: It is Gen. Pete Quesada's notion that not only was the $2.1 million outlay he made for 28 American League players in last winter's grab-bag not a holdup, but that each new club got its money's worth. . . . "Right now, if it were possible under baseball rules, I could pick up the phone and sell half a dozen of our players for what we paid for the original 28," said the General.

* * *

Jack McDonald in the San Francisco News-Call Bulletin: The Giants traded Bill White to St. Louis for Sam Jones but the current Cardinal first-sacker never resented it. . . . "Owner Horace Stoneham takes good care of his players," White was saying, "and a happy player is necessary to a club's success. . . . The Giants have improved since I left them. . . . I doubt if I could ... make it at first

154 games, Babe Ruth, 60.' The other entry will say, 'Most homers in a season, 162 games.' "

Former Detroit slugger Hank Greenberg, one of only three players to hit as many as 58 homers in a season, also offered an opinion. "I think that Maris has only a slim chance to better the record inside 154 games, and Mantle has none," he said. "However, I expect both to hit 61 or better in 162 games. If that happens, the record will be recognized by the fans."

The combined Maris-Mantle total of 109 home runs already had bettered the single-season teammate record of 107 held by former Yankees Ruth (60) and Lou Gehrig (47) in 1927. And it had accounted for almost half of the Yankees' team total of 219, which was only two short of the major league record shared by the 1947 New York Giants and 1956 Cincinnati Reds. Thanks to that power and the 62-13 combined record of pitchers Whitey Ford, Terry, Luis Arroyo and Jim Coates, the Yankees were 100-45 and their magic number for clinching the A.L. pennant was down to seven.

Yankees Record: 100-45 1st +11½

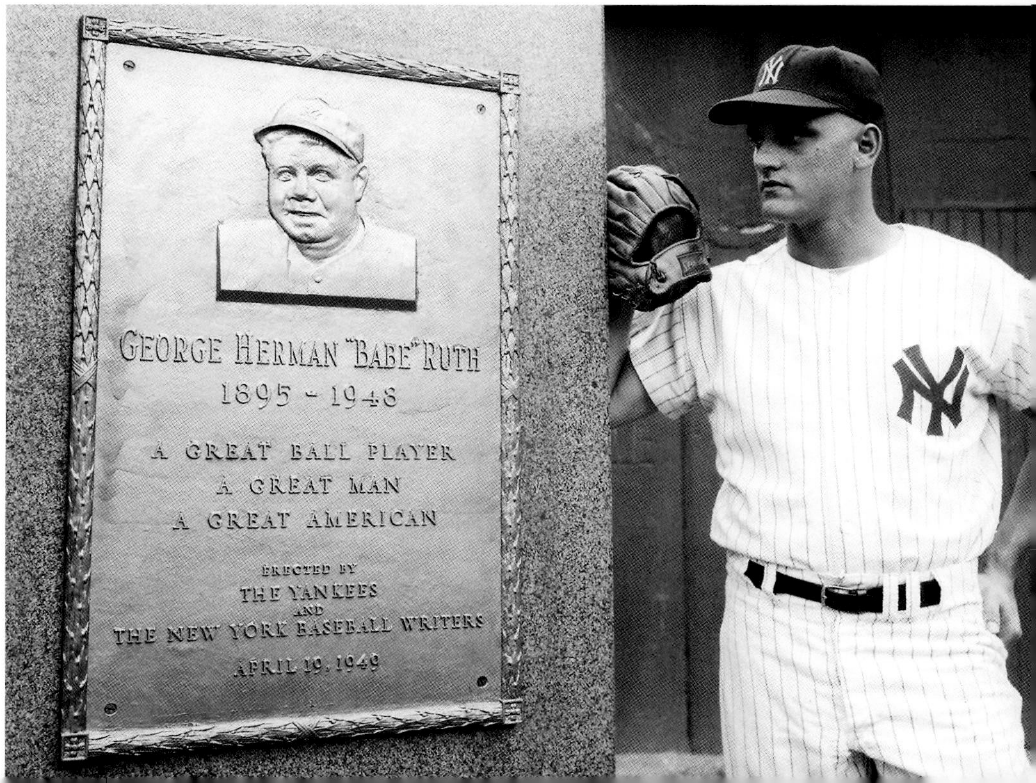
GEORGE HERMAN "BABE" RUTH
1895 - 1948
A GREAT BALL PLAYER
A GREAT MAN
A GREAT AMERICAN
ERECTED BY
THE YANKEES
AND
THE NEW YORK BASEBALL WRITERS
APRIL 19, 1949

By September 10, Babe Ruth was very much a part of Maris' life and Yankee Stadium, the House That Ruth Built, was filled with reminders of the Bambino. Maris (right) posed with the Ruth monument that stood in center field for many years.

WEEK 23		HOME RUN	ON BASE	INN.	OPPONENT (H) OR (A)	PITCHER (THROWS)	GAME	PACE	RUTH'S PACE
SEPT. 14		–	–	–	CHICAGO (A)		147		
		–	–	–	CHICAGO (A)		148		
SEPT. 15		–	–	–	DETROIT (A)		149		
		–	–	–	DETROIT (A)		150		
SEPT. 16	MARIS	57	1	3	DETROIT (A)	LARY (RH)	151	62	57
SEPT. 17	MARIS	58	1	12	DETROIT (A)	FOX (RH)	152	62	58
SEPT. 18					OFF DAY				
SEPT. 19		–	–	–	BALTIMORE (A)		153		
		–	–	–	BALTIMORE (A)		154		
SEPT. 20	MARIS	59	0	3	BALTIMORE (A)	PAPPAS (RH)	155	62	60

Mantle fades, but Maris continues his run at Babe Ruth's record

◆
WEEK

23

September 14-20

The countdown was on. Nine games remaining in commissioner Ford Frick's "154 games or bust" home run edict. ... a magic number of seven for the Yankees to clinch their 26th American League pennant. ... 17 games left in the expanded 162-game schedule. And, for Mickey Mantle, a few more painful swings in his quest for home run immortality.

"I can't make it, not even in 162 games," Mantle said after going hitless in a September 14 doubleheader loss at Chicago that ended the Yankees' 13-game winning streak. "I figure if I could have hit a couple here, I might have been able to do it. But I don't think I can do it now."

There was more to Mantle's resignation than met the eye. A few days earlier, the center fielder had gone to a doctor for a shot that supposedly would knock out a nagging virus. It did a lot more than that. The needle hit a bone in his hip and Mantle ended up in the hospital with a 104-degree temperature and a whole set of complications that included an infected side that eventually had to be lanced and drained.

But Mantle refused to sit down. With 53 home runs, three behind outfield mate Roger Maris with the clock ticking on Frick's 154-game decree, he continued his quest. Several times during the week he came

As the 154-game deadline neared, stress mounted on would-be home run king Roger Maris (above) in his daily dealings with the media.

close to home runs—one drive at Detroit was pulled back into the park by right fielder Al Kaline—but he finally ran out of gas. Too sick to play in a September 19 doubleheader at Baltimore, he watched Game 154 (the Yankees' 155th because of an April tie) the next day from the sideline.

Mantle's concession did not sit well with Maris, who seemed overwhelmed at the thought of facing the media frenzy without his friend and roommate. Maris also had failed to connect in the Chicago doubleheader and entered a Friday doubleheader at Detroit needing four home runs in seven games to tie Babe Ruth's 154-game record of 60.

"I may not do a thing here over the weekend," Maris told reporters, "but I'm going to keep on thinking I may break the record until I have exhausted every chance. Mickey is too good a hitter, too great a competitor to have conceded. I don't think he's out of it at all. No sir. I don't count myself out and I can't count out Mickey."

Nothing captured the exasperation of countdown week more than that Detroit series. Maris finished the Friday doubleheader with one hit in nine at-bats—a second-game single—and then spent the postgame period hidden away in the Yankee trainer's room, which was off limits to the media. "Maris Sulks in Trainer's Room As Futile Night Changes Mood," read the next-day headline in the *New York Times*.

The story went on to chide Maris for his reticence and it quoted a team spokesman as saying he was tired of "being ripped by writers in every city." But manager Ralph Houk revealed later that Maris was holed up in the trainer's room talking to his brother Rudy, who had come to Detroit to watch him play. The flap resounded throughout the country.

And the next day, after going seven games without a home run, Maris' bat resounded once again when he hit homer No. 57, a two-run, third-inning drive off Detroit righthander Frank Lary.

"That was a big one for Roger," Houk said after watching his team lose, 10-4. "Psychologically, it should do him a world of good."

"Roger needed a homer today," Mantle agreed. "He got it and I think it will give him a big lift. I also think he has a helluva shot at the record. If he can get another one here tomorrow, he'll go into Baltimore needing only two to tie, three to beat Ruth's 60 within the 154-game deadline set by commissioner Ford Frick."

Home run ball 57 bounced off the slanted right field roof at Tiger Stadium and was returned to Maris by Kaline. Home run ball 58 disappeared the next day into the right-center field stands—a spectacular 400-foot drive in the top of the 12th inning off Terry Fox that gave the Yankees a 6-4 victory and reduced their magic number to two. Maris' home run was made possible, ironically, when an error by first baseman Bill Skowron helped the Tigers score two runs in the eighth to force extra innings.

"I thought first that these were two runs that would put us ahead of the Tigers," Maris said after becoming only the fourth player to hit 58 home runs in a season. "When I stepped on home plate, I thought about having hit my 58th homer. Now in the dressing room, a half hour later,

Maris (opposite page) drives a pitch from Detroit's Frank Lary toward the right field bleachers of Tiger Stadium and then pauses in the batter's box (above) to watch the flight of his 57th home run.

Maris delivered home run No. 58 in the 12th inning of a dramatic September 17 game against Detroit with Mantle kneeling in the on-deck circle (opposite page). Maris' mood was contemplative (right) after drawing a first-inning walk from Steve Barber in the opener of a September 19 doubleheader at Baltimore—game No. 153.

I'm thinking about what a great thrill it is to know that I'm second to Babe Ruth."

Maris barely missed another home run when his seventh-inning triple bounced off the top of the right-center field wall, about a foot from home run territory. With an off day Monday, a scheduled doubleheader at Baltimore Tuesday and Game 154 (Frick's D-Day) Wednesday, he clearly had momentum on his side.

But that would change—quickly. Off-day rumors that Maris had asked Houk for Tuesday off because of the suffocating pressure drew a quick denial from Houk, who told reporters "he very definitely will be playing in this series." Then Maris went a disappointing 1-for-8 in the doubleheader against tough lefthander Steve Barber, who outpitched

Whitey Ford in a 1-0 opener, and knuckleballers Hal Brown and Hoyt Wilhelm, who pitched well in the nightcap although the Yankees posted a 3-1 win and clinched a tie for the pennant. With 31,317 Baltimore fans cheering his every move on a windy, gloomy day, Maris never came close to a home run.

"As far as Mr. Frick is concerned, I have only one game left to break Babe Ruth's home run record," Maris said after the second game. "But as far as I'm concerned, I have nine games left, at least physically."

Yankees Record: 104-50   1st   +10

154

Valiant Maris effort falls one homer short

Sweat dripped from his face and his smile was tired and forced. Roger Maris, pinned against the clubhouse wall, barely spoke above a whisper as a semicircle of reporters inched ever closer, straining to wring every ounce of emotion from his guarded words. For those few who looked closely, the real story was in his eyes—a tale of pride, disappointment and ultimate relief.

"I am glad that we have played game No. 154 and that from now on I will hit under less tension," he admitted to the frenzied throng. "Yes, there has been tension. Now I feel free and relaxed. I have no squawks. I'm happy."

Maris was speaking as the second most prolific home run hitter in baseball history. Moments earlier, his valiant effort to match Babe Ruth's 1927 home run record of 60 had fallen one short in Baltimore, the city where the Bambino was born more than six decades earlier. This was the Yankees' 154th game played to a decision—the end of the season for anybody who wanted to top Ruth's single-season home run record under the "official" definition provided by commissioner Ford Frick. ABC was broadcasting it to a national audience. Reporters and broadcasters had converged from all over the country to witness it. Maris' team was trying to win it and clinch its 26th American League pennant.

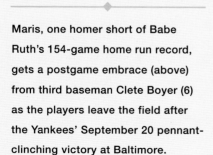

Maris, one homer short of Babe Ruth's 154-game home run record, gets a postgame embrace (above) from third baseman Clete Boyer (6) as the players leave the field after the Yankees' September 20 pennant-clinching victory at Baltimore.

"I tried hard all night, but I only got one," said Maris, who had entered the game with 58 home runs. "Now that it's over, I'm happy with what I got. From now on I'll concentrate on straightening myself out ... for the World Series. Commissioner Frick makes the rules. If all I will be entitled to will be an asterisk, it will be all right with me."

On the scoreboard at upper right:

P
WASH

I
K C
CLEV   0 0
L A   3 6
DETR

UMPIRE PLATE

With time running out on Maris' record chase, he connects (above) off Baltimore righthander Milt Pappas. Home run No. 59 gave Maris distinction as the second player to reach that single-season plateau.

For pure theater, home run No. 59 was hard to beat. It was delivered with perfect timing by a fascinating character on a national stage. Maris' bases-empty blow in the third inning off Orioles righthander Milt Pappas not only lifted him to within one of Ruth's record, it gave even more meaning, drama and intensity to a game that already rated high in all three categories.

Maris' drive into the right field bleachers was impressive. To get there, the ball had to cut through a gusting pitcher's wind that challenged every would-be home run on a damp, chilly Baltimore evening. The eyes of the baseball world were focused squarely on Memorial Stadium when it sailed over the 380-foot marker and landed in a mass of souvenir-hunting humanity.

Suddenly, what had seemed like a hopeless dream transformed into gripping drama. Maris, who had flied to right in the first inning, was now the second player in history to hit 59 home runs in a season. He

There was reason to celebrate for (above, left to right) Luis Arroyo, Maris, Ralph Houk and Whitey Ford after the Yankees clinched their 26th pennant. Maris (below) meets with Bob Reitz, the Orioles fan who caught his 59th home run. Reitz elected to keep the historic ball.

would get two or three more at-bats in a regulation game and every swing would be greeted with cutting-edge intensity by 21,032 soggy Baltimore fans.

Maris batted again in the fourth against reliever Dick Hall, a righthander with a herky-jerky motion. The crowd moaned in disbelief when the Yankees right fielder, after hitting a long foul, struck out on a bad pitch. He returned to the plate in the seventh and almost struck gold. First Maris brought the crowd to its feet with a drive down the line that hooked about 10 feet foul into the right field seats. Then he belted a high drive that might have been out on a normal day. But the wind knocked it down and right fielder Earl Robinson caught it in front of the warning track.

Maris would get one more shot. With the Yankees leading 4-2 and on the verge of their pennant-clinching win, he stepped to the plate in the ninth inning to face his worst nightmare—knuckleballer Hoyt Wilhelm.

"I had to do it against the best thrown at me and have no complaint," Maris said later. "I will say this: If Wilhelm's knuckler is under control, you are not going to hoist it out of the park."

The first pitch to Maris hit his bat on a check swing and went foul. Maris was out in front of the second pitch, checked his swing and again the ball hit his bat. This time it rolled fair down the first base line where Wilhelm picked it up and tagged Maris, ending his 154-game crusade.

"I wanted to go out swinging," Maris said, "but I never did get to swing once against Wilhelm."

The Yankees clinched the pennant, Ralph Terry lifted his record to 15-3 and the celebration began. But while champagne flowed through most of the clubhouse, Maris played host to a different kind of party while pinned to the wall, being grilled by hungry questioners.

"If what I can do from now on cannot count toward an official record, there's no sense in yapping," he said. "I had my chance and I didn't quite make it. I do wish those close foul drives in the fourth and seventh innings after No. 59 had gone a bit over to the left.

"But, hey, I'm happy. My wife called me from home and said that she had seen me hit No. 59 over TV."

Maris (above) found reason to smile while talking about his failure to catch Ruth. He also took consolation in the news that wife Pat (right) was able to watch his 59th home run on a special ABC-TV hookup in the Kansas City area.

WEEK 24		HOME RUN	ON BASE	INN.	OPPONENT (H) OR (A)	PITCHER (THROWS)	GAME	PACE	RUTH'S PACE
SEPT. 21		–	–	–	BALTIMORE (A)		156		
SEPT. 22					OFF DAY				
SEPT. 23	MANTLE	54	2	1	BOSTON (A)	SCHWALL (RH)	157	56	–
SEPT. 24		–	–	–	BOSTON (A)		158		
SEPT. 25					OFF DAY				
SEPT. 26	MARIS	60	0	3	BALTIMORE (H)	FISHER (RH)	159	62	–
SEPT. 27		–	–	–	BALTIMORE (H)		160		

Move over Babe, there's a new guy sharing your home run throne

WEEK

24

September 21-27

It was supposed to get easier. With the 154-game albatross removed from his neck, Roger Maris could relax, regain his perspective and resume his quest to become the most prolific single-season home run hitter in baseball history.

"I thought the pressure would be off me after the 154th game," Maris confided to reporters on an open date, five days after hitting his 59th home run in a dramatic contest at Baltimore. "But I was wrong. It's worse than ever now. The way things are going, I don't even think I'll hit 60 homers by the end of the season, even though I've got five games left, all in New York."

Maris' anguish, growing with every homerless at-bat, was largely self-inflicted. Some of the media clamor had diminished after his failure to reach Babe Ruth's 60-homer mark in game 154 and fans seemed generally resigned to the notion that the Great Home Run Chase was over. But smaller crowds, reduced expectations and gloating critics seemed only to increase his desire to go where only one other home run hitter had gone before.

"Roger's exhaustion isn't physical," Yankees manager Ralph Houk told *New York Times* columnist Arthur Daley. "It's mental, with never a moment of peace in the last month. It's all new to him. He hasn't been trained for it. ... Roger has handled himself beautifully under this con-

With time running out on the season and Roger Maris' quest for 60 home runs, the pressure continued to mount. Maris (center) gets consoling words from former Yankees great Phil Rizzuto (right).

stant pressure. He's been living in a madhouse and my admiration for him has steadily increased."

Houk's "admiration" wasn't shared by everybody. After Maris had failed to reach the 60-homer plateau by commissioner Ford Frick's 154-game deadline, sports columnists throughout the nation rejoiced that "Old Babe's" 34-year-old record was safe from a "colorless, journeyman player who had never batted .300 in his career." Even *The Sporting News* seemed to be writing an obituary on the home run race with an editorial that read, "In the final days of his assault on the record, Maris received much criticism for a petulant attitude, for complaining about various matters and resenting the intrusion of the press. On the final day, however, Maris made many friends for himself by his determined attitude. He gave it all he had and it is a tribute to him and to Baltimore that Oriole fans, loyal to their native son Babe, gave Maris a standing ovation at the end."

The "relaxed" Maris failed to connect in the Yankees' final game at Baltimore and each of the next two games at Boston. After the off day, he was joined by wife Pat in New York for the final leg of his quest,

Mantle ends 1961 season in hospital

Closure in the 1961 home run race came prematurely for Mickey Mantle, who spent his final 1961 regular-season games swinging, running and competing in considerable pain. At first the Yankees center fielder was sidelined by a stubborn viral infection. By season's end, he was in the hospital, wondering how a bout with the flu had turned into a painful abscessed hip.

Mantle, who had not hit a home run since September 10, was limited to one pinch-hit appearance in the four-game September 19-21 Baltimore series because of the flu. But he made a surprise return to the lineup September 24 in Boston, his first start in a week, and responded with typical Mantle dramatics. He crashed his career-best 54th home run, a three-run first-inning shot off Don Schwall, and helped Whitey Ford raise his record to 25-4.

Mantle was 0-for-3 the next day against Boston and started in center field September 26 against Baltimore. But that would be it. He was forced to the locker room after one inning of that game and missed watching teammate Roger Maris hit his 60th home run.

"It's really nothing serious," Yankees manager Ralph Houk told reporters the next day. "Mostly, he's suffering from the aftereffects of the medication he received when hit with the virus in Baltimore. He should be all right for the Red Sox series."

But on September 28, an off day, the mood was not so optimistic. Mantle had been taken to the hospital, where doctors incised and packed the abscess. He would remain there for the last three days of the regular season.

which would begin against a Baltimore pitching staff that had surrendered two home runs to him in 17 games. There were only 19,401 fans on hand for the Tuesday night opener when Orioles righthander Jack Fisher matched pitches with Bud Daley.

But what the crowd lacked in quantity, it more than made up for with intensity. The fans roared when Maris stepped to the plate in the first inning and singled. Then, in the third, Yankee Stadium turned to bedlam when Maris drove a two-out Fisher pitch into the right field third deck just inside the foul pole, placing his name, at last, alongside the immortal Ruth.

Maris, who stood momentarily in the batter's box to watch his majestic drive, trotted casually around the bases before being mobbed in the Yankees dugout by jubilant teammates. After much prodding, Maris moved to the top step for a well-deserved tip of the cap—just as the ball, which

Whether signing autographs for young fans (below, opposite page) or waiting for his next at-bat in the on-deck circle, the burden of the Bambino never escaped Maris' thoughts. When he finally hit his 60th home run on September 26 (above), he matched the feat accomplished only by the immortal Babe Ruth (right) in 1927.

crashed off an upper-deck seat, bounced back onto the field and was retrieved by right fielder Earl Robinson, was rolled into the dugout.

"This is easily the greatest thrill of my life," an emotional Maris said after the game. "I stood and watched the ball because I wanted to make sure it stayed fair. I don't know what to say, how to tell you what I feel. I was in a fog. I don't remember what anyone said to me. All I know is that I'm happy."

Maris flied to right in the fifth and seventh innings, his final two at-bats. Yankee fans, their team leading 3-2, rooted heartily for the Orioles to tie the game in the eighth and ninth so he could get another shot at 61, but the Bronx Bombers held on for their 106th victory.

There were plenty of reasons to smile after Maris joined Ruth on the magical 60-homer plateau. Maris (top photo) shows the ball he crashed off an upper-deck seat and he takes time (right) for a celebratory hug with wife Pat. Orioles righthander Jack Fisher (above) was Maris' 60th victim.

Maris, obviously relieved after weeks of strain, leans back in his locker and holds up the congratulatory telegrams from friends and other well-wishers.

On hand for the historic moment was Claire Ruth, the Babe's widow, who appeared on broadcaster Red Barber's postgame show and congratulated Maris on his home run, which landed about 40 feet to the right of the spot where Ruth's 60th had landed in 1927. But missing were many of the sportswriters who had already dismissed Maris' 60th as "four games too late."

Having reached the Ruthian pinnacle and not thrilled by the prospect of facing tough lefthander Steve Barber September 27, Maris created a new storm by taking a day off.

"I certainly think Roger is entitled to a day off," Houk said. "He's been through a pretty rough ordeal. I think that with this day off and our Thursday open date, he'll be that much better for our final series with the Red Sox."

New York writers were stunned that Maris, going for the ultimate of baseball records, would choose not to play with four games remaining in the season. But Maris was "too bushed" to care. Without that day off, given his frazzled frame of mind, homer No. 61 might never have happened.

Yankees Record: 106-53 1st +8

WEEK 25	HOME RUN	ON BASE	INN.	OPPONENT (H) OR (A)	PITCHER (THROWS)	GAME	PACE	RUTH'S PACE
SEPT. 28				OFF DAY				
SEPT. 29	–	–	–	BOSTON (H)		161		
SEPT. 30	–	–	–	BOSTON (H)		162		
OCTOBER 1 MARIS	61	0	4	BOSTON (H)	STALLARD (RH)	163	61	–

61 in '61: Maris becomes homer king on final day of season

◆
WEEK

25

September 28 - October 1

It was hard to believe. With the American League-champion Yankees closing out an amazing regular season, Whitey Ford going for his 26th victory and Roger Eugene Maris on the verge of baseball history, the last three games at Yankee Stadium drew 63,700 fans—fewer than had attended a September 1 game against Detroit.

And many of them were positioned in the right field sector of the park, hoping they could catch Maris' 61st home run ball and earn a quick $5,000 from Sam Gordon—a publicity-minded Sacramento, Calif., restaurateur who had offered a bounty for the historic souvenir.

This was cooldown week, the calm before the World Series storm— an annual rite of fall in New York. The luster of Maris' crusade to become the first player ever to hit 61 home runs in a season and top Babe Ruth's record had been tarnished by commissioner Ford Frick's 154-game ultimatum, the Yankees had long-since clinched their 11th A.L. pennant in 13 years and Mickey Mantle was lying in a hospital bed, no longer a factor in the two-headed home run race. The "battle of 61" was a reference to Maris' fragile state of mind.

"I think these two days off have done me a lot of good," he said on the eve of his final three games against Boston. "I feel more relaxed than I have been in some time. I'll be swinging freely and if I'm lucky, well, maybe I'll hit one or two more. Right now, though, I would say the most important job confronting us is the winning of the World Series."

Maris, obviously affected by a nervous meltdown from the intense media scrutiny leading up to his 60th home run on September 26, had

With all eyes focused on his powerful swing, Roger Maris connects with a pitch from Boston's Tracy Stallard (above) and becomes baseball's all-time single-season home run champion.

decided to sit out the next day against Baltimore—a decision that stunned the New York media. But, combined with a scheduled off day, he returned to Yankee Stadium with head clear and body refreshed. The conclusion to his long journey was at hand.

◆

September 29—Whitey Ford, tuning up for Game 1 of the World Series, worked six innings and did not get the decision in an eventual 2-1 Yankees win. Red Sox righthander Bill Monbouquette walked Maris twice, to a resounding chorus of boos from 21,485 fans, and induced popups in his other two at-bats. Rollie Sheldon picked up the win when

Yankee players (top photo, left to right) Elston Howard, Bill Skowron, Luis Arroyo and Yogi Berra celebrate the 61st home run by Maris (opposite page) and a 109-53 regular-season finish. Maris also is on the mind of Cincinnati manager Fred Hutchinson (above), who has to figure out a way to handle him and the Yankees in the World Series.

Maris walked in the ninth, moved to second on a sacrifice and scored on Johnny Blanchard's single.

◆

September 30—Rookie righthander Don Schwall walked Maris once and got him twice on ground balls to second base. Maris singled in his final at-bat. Ralph Terry worked six innings for the Yankees and was credited with a 3-1 win, his 16th in 19 decisions.

◆

October 1—On a beautiful fall afternoon, with only 23,154 fans at Yankee Stadium, Maris became the first player to top 60 home runs in a season when he lined a 2-0 fourth-inning pitch from righthander Tracy Stallard into the right field bleachers—a solo shot that sent thousands of fans into a predictable frenzy. As hungry souvenir hunters battled for the bouncing ball, Maris circled the bases as the most prolific single-season home run hitter in baseball history, asterisk or no asterisk.

The home run, fittingly, was the only run in the Yankees' 1-0 victory and it made a winner of Bill Stafford, who worked six innings in a World Series tuneup before giving way to relievers Hal Reniff and Luis Arroyo. Maris flied out, struck out and popped out in his other three

Quick Facts

Here are some quick facts about the Roger Maris and Mickey Mantle home run chase:

■ Maris played in 161 of the Yankees' 163 games, sitting out July 29 against Baltimore with a pulled muscle and resting September 27 against the Orioles. In the May 22 game against Baltimore, he played only one inning because of a bad reaction to eye drops. Mantle played 153 games and he appeared in several others only as a pinch hitter. He sat out the final four games and seven of the Yankees' final 11 while battling the flu and an abscess in his side. The Yankees played 163 games because of an April 22 tie against Baltimore.

■ Maris hit 31 of his 61 homers on the road and 49 off righthanded pitchers. Mantle hit 30 of his 54 on the road and 43 from the left side of the plate.

■ Maris finished with a .269 average, tied for the American League lead with 132 runs scored and led the A.L. with 142 RBIs and 366 total bases. Of his 159 hits, only 98 were not home runs. Mantle batted .317, tied Maris with 132 runs and collected four more hits than his teammate in 76 fewer official at-bats.

■ Maris homered 15 times in June, 13 times in July. Mantle's most prolific month was July, when he hammered 14 home runs.

■ Maris hit 13 home runs against Chicago, his favorite team, but only three against Baltimore. Mantle's favorite mark was Washington, which served up 11 home runs. He managed only four off Chicago, Cleveland and Baltimore pitchers.

■ Maris and Mantle combined for 29 home runs against pitchers from the Washington and Los Angeles expansion teams. They hit 20 against the Senators, but only nine against the Angels.

■ Maris' record 61st home run was hit with a 35-inch, 33-ounce bat. "I don't imagine I'll be using this bat again," he said.

at-bats before settling into his now-familiar postgame question-and-answer routine.

"As fast as we could get into the locker room, the press was swarming everywhere," recalls Tom Tresh, a late-season Yankees callup in 1961. "It was chaos. Roger's locker was across from mine and there were press people everywhere."

And everyone wanted to know one thing: Did he or didn't he?

"Whether I beat Ruth's record or not is for others to say," Maris told reporters. "But it gives me a wonderful feeling to know that I'm the only man in history to hit 61 home runs. Nobody can take that away from me."

Maris' home run simply punctuated one of the great team efforts in baseball history. The Yankees finished with an incredible 109-53 record and an eight-game bulge over second-place Detroit. They also hit a team-record 240 homers—115 by Maris (61) and Mantle (54) and 92 more by Bill Skowron (28), Yogi Berra (22), Elston Howard (21) and Johnny Blanchard (21).

Howard, who battled for the A.L. batting lead much of the season, hit .348 and Mantle finished at .317. Maris finished at .269 after fighting his way through a horrible first month, but he led the league with 142 RBIs. The six-man pitching contingent of Ford (25-4), Terry (16-3), Arroyo (15-5), Stafford (14-9), Sheldon (11-5) and Jim Coates (11-5) finished a combined 61 games over .500 at 92-31.

Yankees Record: 109-53 1st +8

It was a typical swing, not unlike the hundreds he had taken during a long grueling season. But there was nothing ordinary about the crack of the bat, the sudden roar of expectancy and the white blur that rocketed toward baseball history. With time running down on his destiny, with frayed nerves exposed and emotions running on empty, Roger Maris had ascended to the home run throne that not even Babe Ruth could take from him.

"Babe Ruth was a big man in baseball, maybe the biggest ever," Maris said after becoming the first player to hit 61 home runs in a season. "I'm not saying I am of his caliber, but I'm glad to say I hit more than he did in a season. I'd like to have done it in 154 games, but since I didn't, I'm glad now that I did it in 162 games."

Home run No. 61 was delivered with dramatic flair. It came on the final day of the season, on Maris' third-to-last at-bat, in the Yankees' 163rd game—a schedule anomaly created by an early season tie. The drive into the right field bleachers off Boston rookie righthander Tracy Stallard, which produced the only run of the game, was Maris' second home run over the Yankees' final eight games after he had hit No. 59 on September 20, falling one short of Ruth's 154-game record under the deadline set by commissioner Ford Frick.

"Whether I beat Ruth's record or not is for others to say," Maris said. But officially, at least, Ruth remained the 154-game champion and Maris would go into the books as the home run king of the 162-game post-expansion schedule.

The anatomy of Maris' 61st home run: (Clockwise from top left, opposite page) Kneeling in the on-deck circle, hitting the ball, being greeted at home plate by Yogi Berra (8) and the Yankee batboy, in the dugout and back on the field for a tip of the cap.

"Beating Ruth" had been the consuming focus of the 1961 season since Frick's July ruling and Maris took well-deserved pride in his 61st home run, even if it didn't supplant the ghost of the Bambino in the mindset of a baseball-crazy nation. When he connected on a 2-0 pitch from Stallard, only 23,154 fans were in the stands at Yankee Stadium. But they immediately sensed the moment and roared with anticipation as

Maris' 61st home run touched off a mad scramble in the right field bleachers at Yankee Stadium (above) and made a celebrity out of 19-year-old Brooklyn truck driver Sal Durante (right, opposite page), who won the battle for the valuable souvenir. Rookie righthander Tracy Stallard (below, opposite page) was the victim of Maris' historic blow.

the ball settled 15 rows deep into the bleachers, triggering a mad scramble.

What happened next was lost in the emotion of the moment.

"I knew it was gone the minute I hit it," Maris said. "I can't explain how I felt. I don't know what I was thinking as I rounded the bases. My mind was blank."

"I knew he hit the stuffing out of it," Stallard said. "But I didn't think it was going to be a home run. I turned around and then saw the thing going way up. I don't feel badly about it at all. Why should I? The guy hit 60 home runs off a bunch of other pitchers in the league before he got to me today."

Maris shook hands with a young fan as he trotted down the third base line and he was greeted at home plate by teammate Yogi Berra and the Yankees batboy. His ecstatic teammates mobbed him at the top of the dugout and refused to let him step in until he had taken four bows, four tips of his hat, to the roaring fans.

"In those days, photographers were allowed on the field and it was like a stampede—trying to take pictures of him crossing the plate, in front of the dugout," recalled Russ Nixon, a former Maris teammate in Cleveland who was catching the historic game for Boston. "I basically

got out of the way. The Yankee players pushed Maris out. The whole thing might have lasted about five minutes. That was a long time for those days. But there wasn't a lot of celebration. The game just continued."

But the craziness was only beginning. When the Yankees came to bat in the fifth, Maris was hustled out of the dugout to meet Sal Durante, the 19-year-old Brooklyn truck driver who had caught the $5,000 home run ball. They posed for pictures and Maris returned to the game. Reporters, broadcasters and photographers literally swarmed around the ballpark, creating an unmistakable sense of urgency. The atmosphere was highly charged; emotions were running high.

"Just being there, there was electricity and excitement," former teammate Tom Tresh recalled years later. "Especially over the last couple of weeks. Then he hit No. 60, he tied Babe Ruth and the excitement for me really built. It was almost tense; time was running out.

"I don't think the average fan was pulling for Maris. I think they were pulling for (Mickey) Mantle if anybody was going to beat Ruth's record. It was a very difficult situation, but Roger never backed off."

After the game, Maris sat for hours in the locker room, sipping a beer and answering every question as pride dripped from his haggard face.

"Nobody knows how tired I am," he admitted. "Naturally, I'm happy I got past that 60 during the season. And now that the 61st wasn't hit in 154 games, I'm happy. That's the way it was to be and that's the way it is."

Maris homers, Mantle inspires as Yankees win World Series

Like a horse trying to shake off a persistent fly, the New York Yankees swatted away remnants of the Roger Maris and Mickey Mantle home run chase and redirected their attention to a World Series matchup against the Cincinnati Reds. The powerful Yankees had overcome the season-long home run distraction to win their 26th American League pennant and now they were trying to refocus for a run at their 19th championship and ninth in 15 years.

"The Tigers were not our chief problem (during the season)," manager Ralph Houk said. "We had it right in our own midst. The No. 1 hurdle we had to overcome was the Maris-Mantle home run frenzy. As the excitement over the home run drama grew, so my fears increased. Day after day the headlines were Maris or Mantle or home runs. The interviews were Maris or Mantle.

"Day after day, other fine players contributed richly to our success. Some days Maris and Mantle did not figure in the winning attack, but the stories were still about M&M. ... Credit belongs to Maris and Mantle, too. They handled the situation perfectly. There never was a stress on the 'I'."

While Maris longed to bury his record-setting home run spotlight in the shadow of another Yankees World Series victory, Mantle simply wanted to coax a few more performances out of his battered body. Most of the headlines leading up to Game 1 of the fall classic centered on the availability of the switch-hitting center fielder, who had spent the final days of the regular season in the hospital with an abscessed hip.

For Mickey Mantle (left), swinging the bat was a painful proposition in the World Series. He did hit a single in two Series games and got a rousing cheer (above) from Yankee teammates.

"Even if he's half sick," said Yankees outfielder Bob Hale, "he's better than most players." Unfortunately, Mantle was more than half sick. He made a dramatic appearance before the opener at Yankee Stadium and took five batting practice swings, wincing each time in pain. He went to Houk and told him he would have to sit out Game 1.

That didn't faze the Yankees. Whitey Ford, picking right up where he left off in the regular season, stopped the Reds on two hits and recorded a 2-0 victory. The Yankees showed off their power with game-deciding home runs by Elston Howard and Bill Skowron.

One of two Roger Maris World Series hits was a Game 3-ending home run that sailed over the head of Reds right fielder Frank Robinson (top left) and earned a big greeting (left) from the Yankees dugout. Bobby Richardson (top right) had reason to celebrate after collecting nine hits in the five-game victory, as did first-time World Series manager Ralph Houk (above).

After the Reds had fought back for a 6-2 win in Game 2 behind the four-hit pitching of 21-game winner Joey Jay, Mantle and Maris again took center stage when the Series moved to Cincinnati. The gimpy Mantle made his first appearance since September 26 and went 0-for-4 in Game 3, but Maris gave the Yankees a dramatic 3-2 win with a ninth-inning home run off Bob Purkey.

"It was the most damaging blow of the Series," Reds manager Fred Hutchinson said of the Maris home run, his first hit after 10 Series at-bats. "It ruined a fine pitching performance by Bob Purkey and, after the loss, we just couldn't seem to bounce back."

For Maris, it was the 62nd and final home run of his historic season. He would manage only one more Series hit—a Game 5 double—and finish the classic with a .105 average. For Mantle, there would be one harmless single to show for two Series games before he would give up his inspirational effort. But even without much help from their top guns, the 1961 Yankees, who would come to be regarded as one of the greatest teams in baseball history, were too much for the Reds in a five-game mismatch that prompted Hutchinson to admit, "We were overwhelmed."

With Maris and Mantle reduced to supporting status for much of the World Series, Ford stepped up to claim MVP honors—and one of the fall classic's long-standing records. The talented lefthander won two games and extended his World Series scoreless-innings streak to 32, breaking the mark (29) held, ironically, by a former Boston Red Sox lefthander named Babe Ruth.

One emerged from the 1961 shadows as an embittered home run king, unloved, resentful and betrayed by his greatest success.

The other limped into the 1962 sunshine, a wounded hero who would be lovingly embraced by formerly critical fans because of his most celebrated failure.

For Roger Maris and Mickey Mantle, forever linked by destiny and enduring friendship, the postscript to the 1961 home run chase was a dramatic antithesis. It was a career-deflating personal struggle, both mentally and physically, as Maris tried to cope with unwanted celebrity . . . and it was an ego-building embrace from formally dispassionate fans as Mantle gained status alongside Babe Ruth, Lou Gehrig and Joe DiMaggio as a New York icon.

Maris never again would approach his home run prowess of 1961 and his celebrity would fade into a blur of media rifts, unfair criticism, fan disfavor, injuries and diminishing enthusiasm for the game. Mantle never again would hit more than 35 home runs in a season, but his popularity would grow with every painful swing.

By the end of 1966, Maris' New York association would be over—baseball's home run king traded to St. Louis for a journeyman third baseman named Charlie Smith. By the end of 1968, both Maris and Mantle would be gone from baseball—one headed for post-career seclusion and the other for Hall of Fame glory.

◆

If you look strictly at the numbers, Roger Maris was a critical success in 1962. He hit only 33 homers, but he drove in 100 runs, helped the Yankees win their 27th pennant and played a big part in their dramatic seven-game World Series win over San Francisco. It was his defensive

For Roger Maris (left), there were fewer reasons to smile in a Yankee career that stretched five more seasons after 1961. Mickey Mantle (above) continued his love affair with New York fans for the rest of his life.

play on a Game 7 Willie Mays double in the ninth inning that saved Ralph Terry's 1-0 victory and ensured the Yanks' 20th championship.

But there was little else about 1962 that Maris enjoyed.

"He'll have to be able to handle the pressure, because he's going to have plenty of it," predicted DiMaggio, who had gone through a similar experience after a 1941 season in which he hit in a record 56 straight games. "He'll have more pressure on him this year than he did last summer when he was closing in on the Bambino's home run record."

"He'll have to be able to handle the pressure, because he's going to have plenty of it." —JOE DIMAGGIO

For Maris, that must have seemed impossible. He had survived the swarming media, dealt with daily insults from Ruth and Mantle fans, overcome the daily home run-hitting pressure and read stories about Yankee management and players, his own teammates, who wanted Mantle, not him, to break the record. How could it get worse? Maris would find out quickly.

After a postseason trip to Sacramento—a favor for young New York fan Sal Durante, who was to receive $5,000 for the 61 home run ball—Maris was blasted by local and New York writers for being surly and uncooperative. When he traveled to Milwaukee to accept a postseason award, he remained long after the ceremony signing autographs—and was ripped for leaving the program early. Every refused request was a slap in somebody's face, innocent comments were twisted and every minor misstep was magnified. When Maris arrived in Fort Lauderdale for spring training, he was greeted by uncomplimentary stories from local and wire service writers with whom he had not even talked.

The coup de grace might have been delivered by Hall of Fame second baseman Rogers Hornsby, an outspoken Ruth contemporary who had criticized Maris during the home run chase as a "lousy hitter who had to be awfully lucky to hit 61 homers." When a photographer brought Hornsby, a New York Mets coach, across the diamond to pose with Maris before a spring game, Maris turned his back and walked away. "I didn't want to embarrass a great hitter like Mr. Hornsby by having him pose with a lousy hitter like me," Maris said. "He might have forgotten what he said, but I didn't."

"People hate me for breaking Ruth's record—the press especially." —ROGER MARIS

The Hornsby incident created a furor and Hornsby wouldn't let it die, calling Maris a "bush leaguer" and suggesting his name shouldn't be mentioned in the same sentence with Ruth. Maris was portrayed nationally as an ungrateful villain and New York columnist Jimmy Cannon labeled him "Maris the Whiner", charging that he was jealous of Mantle. Maris responded to all the mounting criticism by issuing a moratorium on interviews—an unwise decision that the New York media took as a challenge. The Yankees right fielder was a marked man—and, besieged by the New York press and fans who believed every negative thing they read, he sank deeper and deeper into a defiant shell that would define the remainder of his career.

"Sometimes I think it wasn't worth the aggravation," Maris said, looking back on his incredible 1961 season. "Maybe I wouldn't do it over again if I had the chance. I had so many people on my tail. People hate me for breaking Ruth's record—the press especially."

The pressure of 1961 never faded for Maris (left), who played the rest of his career as the 'sullen home run king.' Mantle (below) rounds third in a 1968 game against Detroit after hitting his 535th homer, the second-to-last of his Hall of Fame career.

Mickey Mantle did not break Ruth's record—and he never mounted a serious challenge through the remainder of his injury-plagued career. But nobody hated The Mick after 1961, not anymore, and he played the remainder of his career as something of a folk hero. The man who couldn't buy a New York ovation for 10 years suddenly transformed into a living legend, secure at last with those lofty—and sometimes unreasonable—expectations of greatness.

Maris deserves some of the credit for that turnaround, the villainous foil for Mantle's heroics. But the injuries—the knee, groin, leg, foot, shoulder and arm problems that dogged Mantle from his first day as a major leaguer—also played a major role. After watching Mantle struggle valiantly in 1961 to overcome injuries, after seeing his dogged determination

to stay in the lineup and the home run chase, fans who had not appreciated his efforts before suddenly saw him as a baseball warrior.

"I always knew he was bandaged," said former shortstop Dick Howser after joining the Yankees in 1967. "I thought he just wrapped the usual Ace bandage around his leg. Then I saw him wrap all that wide, foam rubber bandage around his legs and couldn't believe it. I wondered how he not only could play bandaged like that, but run as he did.

"After that, I saw little things that made me realize the pain he had. I often saw him pull into second base and grimace. He never complained, nor said a word, but seeing him grimace was enough."

Mantle never played more than 144 games in a season after 1961, but he remained the inspirational centerpiece of the Yankees for seven more seasons. The Yanks won American League pennants in 1962, '63 and '64, stretching their latest streak to five, and ran the franchise championship total to 20. Mantle sparked the Yankees' final charge in 1964 when he batted .303 with 35 homers and 111 RBIs, despite missing 19 games with various ailments.

While the monster seasons diminished, the memorable moments kept coming. One came in 1963, when Mantle was called to pinch hit in a game against Baltimore at Yankee Stadium. It was his first appearance in two months after breaking his foot and the crowd gave him a stirring ovation. Choking back the emotion and just trying to make contact, he hit the first pitch over the left-center field fence.

Choking back the emotion... he hit the first pitch over the left-center field fence.

Another moment, the one Mantle often cited as his favorite, came in 1964, the last of 12 World Series in which he would play. Batting in the ninth inning of a 1-1 Game 3 at Yankee Stadium, Mantle connected with a pitch from Cardinals reliever Barney Schultz for a dramatic home run.

But the Yankees lost to the Cardinals in that seven-game Series and the long championship dynasty finally began to crumble. They fell to sixth place in 1965 and finished last a year later as key players either retired or were traded. Mantle hung on through 1968, but averages of .255, .288, .245 and .237 from 1965-68 belied the inevitable. The spirit was

willing, but the body could no longer answer the call.

Mantle announced his retirement in spring training of 1969 and left with a .298 career average, 536 home runs and 1,509 RBIs. Despite his infirmities, he had played in 2,401 games, more than any player in Yankees history.

On June 8, 1969, an emotional party was held at Yankee Stadium. With 61,000 fans screaming their approval, "Mickey Mantle Day" was celebrated with the retirement of uniform No. 7 and a special plaque giving The Mick equal status with his superstar predecessors.

"I've always wondered how a man who was dying could stand here and say he was the luckiest man in the world," an emotional Mantle told the cheering throng. "Now I know how Lou Gehrig felt."

◆

Maris hit 133 homers, drove in 354 runs and claimed two A.L. MVP awards over the three-season span from 1960-62. His Yankee teams won three pennants and two World Series. He played Gold Glove-caliber defense in his natural right field position and he adjusted smoothly to center when filling in for the ailing Mantle.

And still they booed. Maris' biggest problem was that he couldn't charm the masses like the effervescent Ruth, he didn't exude the

Injuries (left page) were an unfortunate part of Mantle's New York career, which was celebrated in 1969 (right) during Yankee Stadium ceremonies to retire his uniform number. Mantle (top photo) takes time for a few words of advice from former Yankees great Joe DiMaggio and then passes along a few words of his own (above) to 5-year-old David, one of his four sons.

dignity and grace of the stately DiMaggio and he didn't possess the awe-inspiring power or disarming smile of the happy-go-lucky Mantle. Madison Avenue, he was not.

Feuding with the press and suspicious of New York fans, Maris struggled through an injury-plagued 1963 campaign and dropped off to 26 homers and 71 RBIs in 1964. But Maris' worst nightmare was still ahead. The 1965 and '66 seasons would test his love for baseball and stretch him to the point of leaving the game.

"They have finally forgotten 1961," Maris said optimistically in the spring of '65, looking forward to better relations with Yankee fans. "I had two ordinary years and they have forgotten the homers. This year, I'm going to enjoy playing. I hope no one bothers me."

On April 28, while making a spectacular catch in a game against Kansas City, Maris suffered a severely pulled muscle that kept him out of the lineup for 26 games. Shortly after his return, Maris dislocated a finger that sidelined him for four more games. The season really fell apart when he felt something pop in his hand while swinging at a pitch.

Maris was in pain, but the Yankees kept telling reporters the injury was minor. Day after day he watched from the sideline, in constant pain and confused why team doctors couldn't find anything wrong. Soon the inevitable malingering rumors began floating through the clubhouse and streets of New York and writers labeled him a laggard and loafer. Tired of the innuendo and suspicion, Maris demanded a diagnosis from the Yankees, who finally admitted there was damage in his hand that would require surgery. The operation, they said three months after the injury, could cost him full use of his hand—permanently.

"I was living a fairy tale for a while. ...Too bad it ended so badly." –ROGER MARIS

The revelation was startling. But the public relations damage had already been done and Maris, again, was a target of Yankee fans who already were agitated by the prospect of watching a second-division team. After another injury-plagued season in 1966, Maris was ready to retire—until the Yankees

The final two years of Maris' career were spent in St. Louis (left page, above), where he found peace while helping the Cardinals win two National League pennants. 'Family man' Maris was honored (below) by the Cardinals after announcing his retirement in 1968.

informed him he had been traded to St. Louis.

"My going after the record started off as such a dream," said Maris, who vowed never to return to Yankee Stadium. "I was living a fairy tale for a while. I never thought I'd ever get a chance to break such a record. Too bad it ended so badly."

Free from the relentless New York scrutiny, Maris played two enjoyable seasons for the Cardinals. He hit only 14 more homers and drove in 100 runs, but there was little of the pressure that had tortured him for most of his Yankees career. The Cardinals appreciated his solid defense and clutch hitting en route to consecutive National League pennants and a World Series victory.

Maris, still bothered by his hand and other nagging injuries, announced his retirement during the 1968 season and was honored by the Cardinals on September 29 in ceremonies at Busch Memorial Stadium. He left the game after 12 major league seasons with a career .260 average and 275 home runs. The 1961 home run record will endure as his legacy, but baseball insiders point to the seven pennant winners and the three World Series champions for which he played.

"A lot of people remember the home runs, but he was a great ballplayer and a great family man," said former Yankees manager Ralph Houk. "He was modest and winning came above any personal statistic."

◆

Roger Maris kept his promise for almost a decade. He refused to return to Yankee Stadium, mindful of the boos he had once heard and fearful

of the reception he might receive from still-vengeful New York fans. Maris, who had retired to Gainesville, Fla., where he operated a beer distributorship, finally relented in 1978 at the urging of Yankees owner George Steinbrenner.

"Roger was a most misunderstood young man," Steinbrenner said. "In my mind, the Yankees (under then-owners Del Webb and Dan Topping) treated him shabbily. He should have been a hero. To me, Roger Maris was one of the greatest Yankees of all time. And that's a mouthful, because there are so many of them."

Maris had turned down Old-Timers Day invitations for years, but he finally was persuaded by Steinbrenner to join Mantle on opening day in 1978 for the raising of the team's 1977 championship banner. The scene was electric as Maris, with the tape of his 61st homer playing on the scoreboard, was introduced by the voice of longtime broadcaster Mel Allen saying, "Welcome Back Roger." Fans screamed and shouted his name in a tribute that obviously moved the emotional home run champion.

He returned again ... and again for Old-Timers festivities, the most memorable in 1984. With the widow of former teammate Elston Howard at his side in a July 21 ceremony, Maris' uniform No. 9 and Howard's 32 were retired in a poignant scene recalled by Steinbrenner. "The fans stood and applauded for a good 15 minutes," the Yankees boss said. "That did a lot of good for him."

> ## "The fans stood and applauded for a good 15 minutes." —GEORGE STEINBRENNER

Maris would not enjoy many more special moments at Yankee Stadium. The lymphatic cancer, which had first been diagnosed in

Maris made his first post-retirement return to Yankee Stadium in 1978, where he was reunited with Mantle (above) in ceremonies to raise the team's 1977 championship banner. Maris and the widow of former teammate Elston Howard shared the spotlight in 1984 (left page) when the Yankees retired their uniform numbers 32 and 9.

November 1983, was getting worse. Maris died on December 14, 1985, in a Houston hospital at age 51, secure at last in the appreciation of his baseball legacy.

◆

For Mickey Mantle, there would be many post-retirement moments at Yankee Stadium—ego-boosting reunions with DiMaggio, Whitey Ford, Maris and other former teammates and lovefests with the New York fans who had once made his life so difficult. But his biggest moment, one that eluded Maris, was his 1974 induction, with old pal Ford, into baseball's Hall of Fame at Cooperstown.

Mantle, the man who was so convinced he would not live past age 40, survived his injuries, alcoholism and many other physical indiscretions before succumbing, like Maris, to cancer in 1995. He died, 10 years after his soulmate slugger, at age 63.

Mantle/Maris *a statistical comparison*

HR	GAME DATE	OPPOSING PITCHER	BALL CLUB	HOME/ AWAY	INNING	ON BASE
1	April 17	Jerry Walker (RH)	Kansas City	H	1	1
2	April 20 (1)	Eli Grba (RH)	Los Angeles	H	1	1
3	April 20 (1)	Eli Grba (RH)	Los Angeles	H	5	2
4	April 21	Steve Barber (LH)	Baltimore	A	3	1
5	April 23	Chuck Estrada (RH)	Baltimore	A	4	0
1	April 26	Paul Foytack (RH)	Detroit	A	5	0
6	April 26	Jim Donohue (RH)	Detroit	A	8	1
7	April 26	Hank Aguirre (LH)	Detroit	A	10	1
8	May 2	Camilo Pascual (RH)	Minnesota	A	10	3
2	May 3	Pedro Ramos (RH)	Minnesota	A	7	2
9	May 4	Ted Sadowski (RH)	Minnesota	A	6	0
3	May 6	Eli Grba (RH)	Los Angeles	A	5	0
10	May 16	Hal Woodeshick (LH)	Washington	H	6	0
4	May 17	Pete Burnside (LH)	Washington	H	8	1
5	May 19	Jim Perry (RH)	Cleveland	A	1	1
6	May 20	Gary Bell (RH)	Cleveland	A	3	0
7	May 21	Chuck Estrada (RH)	Baltimore	H	1	0
8	May 24	Gene Conley (RH)	Boston	H	4	1
9	May 28 (2)	Cal McLish (RH)	Chicago	H	2	1
11	May 29	Ike Delock (RH)	Boston	A	7	0
12	May 30	Gene Conley (RH)	Boston	A	1	2
10	May 30	Gene Conley (RH)	Boston	A	3	0
11	May 30	Mike Fornieles (RH)	Boston	A	8	2
13	May 30	Mike Fornieles (RH)	Boston	A	8	0
12	May 31	Billy Muffett (RH)	Boston	A	3	0
14	May 31	Billy Muffett (RH)	Boston	A	4	1
13	June 2	Cal McLish (RH)	Chicago	A	3	2
14	June 3	Bob Shaw (RH)	Chicago	A	8	2
15	June 4	Russ Kemmerer (RH)	Chicago	A	3	0
15	June 5 (1)	Ray Moore (RH)	Minnesota	H	8	2
16	June 6	Ed Palmquist (RH)	Minnesota	H	6	2
17	June 7	Pedro Ramos (RH)	Minnesota	H	3	2
16	June 9	Ray Herbert (RH)	Kansas City	H	3	2
18	June 9	Ray Herbert (RH)	Kansas City	H	7	1
17	June 10	Bill Kunkel (RH)	Kansas City	H	8	0
18	June 11 (2)	Eli Grba (RH)	Los Angeles	H	1	2
19	June 11 (2)	Eli Grba (RH)	Los Angeles	H	3	0
20	June 11 (2)	Johnny James (RH)	Los Angeles	H	7	0
21	June 13	Jim Perry (RH)	Cleveland	A	6	0
22	June 14	Gary Bell (RH)	Cleveland	A	4	1
19	June 15	Mudcat Grant (RH)	Cleveland	A	7	0
23	June 17	Don Mossi (LH)	Detroit	A	4	0
20	June 17	Paul Foytack (RH)	Detroit	A	9	2
24	June 18	Jerry Casale (RH)	Detroit	A	8	1
25	June 19	Jim Archer (LH)	Kansas City	A	9	0
26	June 20	Joe Nuxhall (LH)	Kansas City	A	1	0
21	June 21	Bob Shaw (RH)	Kansas City	A	1	2
22	June 21	Bob Shaw (RH)	Kansas City	A	7	1
27	June 22	Norm Bass (RH)	Kansas City	A	2	1
23	June 26	Ken McBride (RH)	Los Angeles	A	2	0
24	June 28	Ryne Duren (RH)	Los Angeles	A	9	1
25	June 30	Dick Donovan (RH)	Washington	H	6	1
26	July 1	Carl Mathias (LH)	Washington	H	2	0
27	July 1	Carl Mathias (LH)	Washington	H	3	2
28	July 1	Dave Sisler (RH)	Washington	H	9	1
29	July 2	Pete Burnside (LH)	Washington	H	3	2
30	July 2	Johnny Klippstein (RH)	Washington	H	7	1
28	July 2	Johnny Klippstein (RH)	Washington	H	8	1

CATEGORIES	MANTLE	MARIS
vs. RHP	43	49
vs. LHP	11	12
Home	24	30
Away	30	31
at Baltimore	4	1
at Boston	6	4
at Chicago	2	5
at Cleveland	2	5
at Detroit	3	5
at Kansas City	2	4
at Los Angeles	2	2
at Minnesota	4	1
at Washington	5	4
Sunday	12	14
Monday	5	1
Tuesday	8	13
Wednesday	10	12
Thursday	6	3
Friday	7	6
Saturday	6	12
1st inning	14	8
2nd inning	4	2
3rd inning	5	15
4th inning	5	10
5th inning	3	3
6th inning	5	6
7th inning	5	7
8th inning	7	7
9th inning	4	2
10th inning	2	0
12th inning	0	1

CATEGORIES	MANTLE	MARIS
Solo	27	31
Two-run	16	21
Three-run	10	9
Grand slams	1	0
2-HR games	8	7
April	7	1
May	7	11
June	11	15
July	14	13
August	9	11
September	6	9
October	0	1
vs. Orioles	4	3
vs. Red Sox	7	7
vs. White Sox	4	13
vs. Indians	4	8
vs. Tigers	5	8
vs. A's	6	5
vs. Angels	5	4
vs. Twins	8	4
vs. Senators	11	9
Pre-1st All-Star	29	33
Post-2nd All-Star	15	21
Between All-Star	10	7
# of pitchers victimized	43	46
Team record	37-9	40-14

Most frequent victim, Mantle—Eli Grba, L.A.; Joe McClain, Was.; 3 each.

Most frequent victim, Maris—Pete Burnside, Was.; Frank Lary, Det.; Jim Perry, Cle.; 3 each.

Games in which both players homered—14

Number of pitchers victimized by both players in same game—12

Times Maris and Mantle homered back-to-back—4

Number of pitchers who surrendered home runs to both players during season—26

Number of different pitchers who surrendered a home run to at least one of the two players—63

Most home runs given up to the two players combined—5, by Eli Grba and Jim Perry

Pitcher surrendering home runs to both Mantle and Maris pitching for two different teams—Ray Herbert, Kansas City and Chicago

Players finishing third in home run race in 1961—Jim Gentile, Balt. and Harmon Killebrew, Min. (46 each)

Roger Maris (left), Baltimore's Jim Gentile (center) and Minnesota's Harmon Killebrew accounted for 153 home runs in the 1961 season.

HR	GAME DATE	OPPOSING PITCHER	BALL CLUB	HOME/ AWAY	INNING	ON BASE
31	July 4 (2)	Frank Lary (RH)	Detroit	H	8	1
32	July 5	Frank Funk (RH)	Cleveland	H	7	0
29	July 8	Tracy Stallard (RH)	Boston	H	5	0
33	July 9 (1)	Bill Monbouquette (RH)	Boston	H	7	0
34	July 13	Early Wynn (RH)	Chicago	A	1	1
30	July 13	Early Wynn (RH)	Chicago	A	1	0
31	July 14	Juan Pizarro (LH)	Chicago	A	8	0
35	July 15	Ray Herbert (RH)	Chicago	A	3	0
32	July 16	Steve Barber (LH)	Baltimore	A	4	0
33	July 17	Milt Pappas (RH)	Baltimore	A	6	0
34	July 18	Joe McClain (RH)	Washington	A	1	1
35	July 18	Joe McClain (RH)	Washington	A	8	0
36	July 19 (2)	Dick Donovan (RH)	Washington	A	6	0
36	July 21	Bill Monbouquette (RH)	Boston	A	1	0
37	July 21	Bill Monbouquette (RH)	Boston	A	1	0
37	July 25 (1)	Frank Baumann (LH)	Chicago	H	4	1
38	July 25 (1)	Frank Baumann (LH)	Chicago	H	4	0
38	July 25 (1)	Don Larsen (RH)	Chicago	H	8	0
39	July 25 (2)	Russ Kemmerer (RH)	Chicago	H	4	0
40	July 25 (2)	Warren Hacker (RH)	Chicago	H	6	2
39	July 26	Ray Herbert (RH)	Chicago	H	1	1
40	Aug. 2 (2)	Art Ditmar (RH)	Kansas City	H	1	1
41	Aug. 4	Camilo Pascual (RH)	Minnesota	H	1	2
41	Aug. 6 (1)	Pedro Ramos (RH)	Minnesota	H	1	1
42	Aug. 6 (1)	Pedro Ramos (RH)	Minnesota	H	3	0
43	Aug. 6 (2)	Al Schroll (RH)	Minnesota	H	2	0
42	Aug. 11	Pete Burnside (LH)	Washington	A	5	0
44	Aug. 11	Pete Burnside (LH)	Washington	A	7	1
43	Aug. 12	Dick Donovan (RH)	Washington	A	4	0
44	Aug. 13 (1)	Bennie Daniels (RH)	Washington	A	4	0
45	Aug. 13 (1)	Bennie Daniels (RH)	Washington	A	9	0
45	Aug. 13 (2)	Marty Kutyna (RH)	Washington	A	1	1
46	Aug. 15	Juan Pizarro (LH)	Chicago	H	4	0
47	Aug. 16	Billy Pierce (LH)	Chicago	H	1	1
48	Aug. 16	Billy Pierce (LH)	Chicago	H	3	1
46	Aug. 20 (1)	Jim Perry (RH)	Cleveland	A	1	2
49	Aug. 20 (1)	Jim Perry (RH)	Cleveland	A	3	1
50	Aug. 22	Ken McBride (RH)	Los Angeles	A	6	1
51	Aug. 26	Jerry Walker (RH)	Kansas City	A	6	0
47	Aug. 30	Jim Kaat (LH)	Minnesota	A	7	0
48	Aug. 31	Jack Kralick (LH)	Minnesota	A	4	0
52	Sept. 2	Frank Lary (RH)	Detroit	H	6	0
53	Sept. 2	Hank Aguirre (LH)	Detroit	H	8	1
49	Sept. 3	Jim Bunning (RH)	Detroit	H	1	1
50	Sept. 3	Gerry Staley (RH)	Detroit	H	9	0
51	Sept. 5	Joe McClain (RH)	Washington	H	2	0
54	Sept. 6	Tom Cheney (RH)	Washington	H	4	0
55	Sept. 7	Dick Stigman (LH)	Cleveland	H	3	0
52	Sept. 8	Gary Bell (RH)	Cleveland	H	5	0
56	Sept. 9	Mudcat Grant (RH)	Cleveland	H	7	0
53	Sept. 10 (2)	Jim Perry (RH)	Cleveland	H	3	0
57	Sept. 16	Frank Lary (RH)	Detroit	A	3	1
58	Sept. 17	Terry Fox (RH)	Detroit	A	12	1
59	Sept. 20	Milt Pappas (RH)	Baltimore	A	3	0
54	Sept. 23	Don Schwall (RH)	Boston	A	1	2
60	Sept. 26	Jack Fisher (RH)	Baltimore	H	3	0
61	Oct. 1	Tracy Stallard (RH)	Boston	H	4	0

New York played 163 games in 1961 (one tie on April 22), with Mantle playing in 153 games and Maris playing in 161 games.

St. Louis slugger Mark McGwire took time from his home run quest to pay respect to the children of Roger Maris, who were invited to St. Louis to watch Big Mac break their father's 37-year-old record. Three Maris boys, (above, left to right) Randy, Kevin and Rich, examine Roger's 61st-home run bat, which was on loan from the Hall of Fame. When McGwire hit his record-breaking homer (opposite page), he climbed into the box seats to share a touching moment with the Maris family (right).

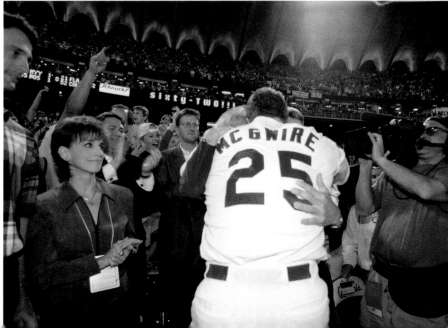

McGwire vs. Sosa —Maris' record finally is broken

It stood as a monument to time, chased but unchallenged for 37 baseball summers. Then, suddenly, in one incredible season, 13 years after Roger Maris' death, the record that had defined his career was obliterated in a blur of Mark McGwire and Sammy Sosa home runs.

Not unlike the 1961 season when Maris and New York Yankees teammate Mickey Mantle chased the home run record of Babe Ruth, St. Louis first baseman McGwire and Chicago Cubs right fielder Sosa waged a prolific battle that ended on the final day of the season with McGwire, incomprehensibly, at 70 and Sosa four back at 66—five more than Maris had hit in his record-setting season.

The record fell during a Labor Day series in St. Louis that pitted the two sluggers in a head-to-head battle. On September 7, McGwire hit No. 61, tying Maris' mark in the Cardinals' 144th game. One day later, Big Mac took his place in the record books when he lined No. 62 down the left field line, touching off the biggest home run celebration in baseball history. After the home run, after hugging his son and Sosa, McGwire climbed over the box-seat railing where the Maris children were sitting and gave their father an emotional, long-overdue salute.

"My body's still numb," Roger Maris Jr. said later. "I'm extremely happy for Mark. For all he's done for baseball ... I couldn't be happier. For Mark to be the person he is and to mean what he means to baseball and to the fans of America, I couldn't think of a better person to be the new home run king for a single season.

"I think Dad would be happy for Mark and proud of him for his accomplishments. He would've been very proud of Mark as a player, but I think more so as a person."

In April 2001, HBO premiered 61*, starring Thomas Jane as Mickey Mantle and Barry Pepper as Roger Maris. The film chronicles the magical 1961 season, in which the two Yankees sluggers competed in the greatest home run race ever staged. Billy Crystal, an avowed New York Yankees fan, discusses making the movie that he produced and directed.

Q: Judging by the attention to detail and events in the movie, you must have a tremendous recollection for that season.

CRYSTAL: I was 13, it was the greatest summer you could imagine being in New York with these two guys. I loved both of them. Mickey clearly was my choice, but I really liked Roger, too. It was a tremendous pennant race, and there was amazing heat on these guys. I had spent so much time in the Stadium (Yankee Stadium) and loved this place so much, I not only remembered way too much, but I also got great footage from the Hall of Fame, Major League Baseball and other sources so that our designer, Rusty Smith, could duplicate that ballpark.

Q: Over the years, you developed a friendship with Mantle. With Bob Costas, you helped write the eulogy that Bob delivered at Mantle's funeral. Did you and Mick talk a lot about that summer?

CRYSTAL: Oh, yeah. I was able to take a lot of things that Mickey told me—things he talked to Roger about and how they interacted in the apartment. We talked many times about the season, the pressure, Roger and what it was like. (Mickey) said to me, "You know, that was the summer that I think, you know, people really started to like me. I don't think they really totally liked me until that season. And then I think they started to like me when it was, like, too late."

Q: Had you ever had the chance to sit and talk to Maris the same way?

CRYSTAL: I never met Roger. But I read so many books, and so many things, and talked to so many people. The greatest compliment I've been given about the movie is when Roger's mother called me and said, "You got it right. How did you know it so well?"

Q: The film begins not with 1961, but with 1998, when Mark McGwire broke Roger Maris' record. Why?

CRYSTAL: I thought it was the way to do it. What caught my eye that day (the day McGwire broke the record), what touched me and made me rework the script, was seeing Mark be so respectful of Roger. And when he hugged the kids in the stands, whom I had met at Mickey's funeral, everybody shed a tear. Everybody was moved by that gesture and the

Actors Barry Pepper (left) and Thomas Jane bear a strong resemblance to Roger Maris and Mickey Mantle, the characters they portray, in the movie 61*.

Jennifer Crystal, who plays Pat Maris, does a scene with Pepper, her movie husband.

thought that Pat (Roger's wife) was in the hospital and not able to get to the game because of the stress and the heart problem that she had.

When HBO approached me about being involved as the producer, I looked at the storyline. It didn't start this way, and I moved the whole story into this because I felt ultimately that 61* was about the loss of a husband and the loss of a father to these kids—that all they had left of him was this record. And, the kids were so young, they didn't even remember, or didn't know, what he went through. That's what touched me, and that's what I think is really powerful and human about the movie. You ultimately feel this nice love story between Roger and Pat.

Q: The two lead actors bear an uncanny resemblance to Roger and Mickey, don't they?

CRYSTAL: They're great. I wanted to discover people in the film. The first time Barry came on screen, in "Saving Private Ryan," I said, "Oh God, there's Roger Maris." Tom didn't know anything about Mickey. I had a beautiful library of photographs, tapes, moments of Mantle's career, interviews, shots of Mickey and I together. He just sat there in my office for hours and I could see he was already under-

standing of how Mickey walked and his neck and his arms ... he just got it. I said to Tom, "I can show you how he held a drink, how he salted his food, how he held a knife and fork." It's down to that kind of stuff.

Q: Large parts of the film were shot at Tiger Stadium. How do you transform Tiger Stadium into Yankee Stadium?

CRYSTAL: That was the blessing of all time. There was only one place, Tiger Stadium in Detroit, and it was a stroke of luck because the Tigers had just moved out. It had the same structure, the same grandeur about it. I remember the date I first went there, on November 19, and it was about 19 below. After we got there, the whole movie just jumped to life. We just mapped out how we physically could change that ballpark into Yankee Stadium and then back to Tiger Stadium, because a lot of things happened in Tiger Stadium. So we painted 55,000 seats, covered them with fabric, the light green that Yankee

Stadium was, and every piece of facade work on the second deck was all us, stuff that we put in. I brought in the right field wall, so it's that great old Yankee Stadium 296, 344. The pillars are treated with plywood that made it look like the deco that Yankee Stadium had back then. The center field wall, the monuments, the 461, that's all us. We built all of that stuff. Everywhere I put the camera, it was Yankee Stadium.

Q: What did you want to accomplish with the movie?

CRYSTAL: I wanted it to be an intimate look at these two men and rivals who became friends. Of Mickey being able to say, "You're a good man, Roger." ... what it was like off the field. I wanted people to come away with a feeling for these two guys that 40 years later people don't know about, and to acquaint them with what it was like for Roger to go through this assault on his character. It's about an interesting time; 1961— JFK, astronauts and the M&M Boys.

Billy Crystal (right) talks things over with Jane (Mantle) on the set of his HBO movie 61*.

Photo Credits

T=TOP   B=BOTTOM   L=LEFT   R=RIGHT   M=MIDDLE

Cover of Roger Maris and Mickey Mantle by Bettmann/Corbis.
Back cover of Maris hitting 59th home run by Bettmann/Corbis.

BETTMANN/CORBIS—4-5, 6, 10, 14, 16, 21, 22, 24B, 27, 29, 30T, 31, 33, 35T, 37T, 36B, 39T, 41B, 43, 44, 45, 47, 48, 48-49, 51, 53T, 53B, 55, 57, 58, 61, 62, 63, 65, 66T, 66B, 66-67, 69, 71TL, 71TM, 71TR, 71B, 75BM, 76T, 76B, 77, 78, 79, 81T, 81B, 82T, 82B, 83T, 85, 87T, 87B, 88T, 88B, 88-89, 91, 92T, 92B, 93T, 93B, 95, 96, 97T, 97B, 98TL, 98TR, 98B, 99, 101T, 101B, 102, 105T, 105B, 106-107, 107B, 108, 109T, 109B, 111, 112, 113T, 113B, 114, 115, 117, 118, 119, 120, 121, 122, 123, 124T, 124B, 125T, 125B, 127, 128T, 128B, 129T, 130T, 130BR, 131, 133, 134B, 135, 136R, 137R, 137B, 138, 139T, 140, 141, 142-143, 142B, 143TR, 143B, 144, 146, 147, 149M, 152, 153.

THE SPORTING NEWS ARCHIVES—12, 12-13, 13T, 13B, 15, 17, 18, 19, 20L, 20R, 23, 24T, 25T, 25B, 30B, 34, 35B, 39M, 39B, 41T, 73, 74TL, 74TM, 74TR, 74BL, 74BR, 75TL, 75TM, 75TR, 75BL, 75BR, 83B, 103, 107T, 129B, 130BL, 134T, 136L, 137TL, 139B, 145, 148, 149T, 149B, 150, 151T, 151B, 154.

COURTESY OF HBO—9, 158, 159T, 159B.